to Sophia
and Demosthenes

Semiotics and Storytelling

BRONWEN MARTIN

SEMIOTICS
and
STORYTELLING

foreword

Dáithí Ó hÓgáin

Semiotics and Storytelling

First paperback edition: **1997**

Published by **Philomel Productions Ltd**, Dublin, Republic of Ireland
for **Philomel-Euromyths, London, U.K.**
Correspondence and contact address: 1, Queen's Gate Place Mews,
London SW7 5BG, U.K.
Tel: ++44 (0)171 581 23 03 / 581 26 73,
Fax: ++44 (0)171 589 22 64

Semiotics and Storytelling by **Bronwen Martin**
Foreword by **Dáithí Ó hÓgáin**
Philomel, the Forest's Nightingale by **Ange S. Vlachos**
Translated by **Sophia Kakkavas**
Illustrated by **Paul S. Vlachos**

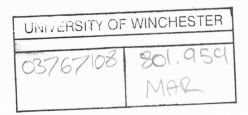
ISBN **1 898685 18 5**

1997

Table of Contents

ALL PROFITS ON SALE OF THIS EDITION GIVEN TO THE EDUCATIONAL PROGRAMME

Philomel

Dáithí Ó hÓgáin

All will agree that the appreciation and evaluation of literature is essential to the advancement of culture and —what is much more to the point— to the quality of life of the individual person. The development of literary art by its nature requires a continuous broadening of horizons, in which original creative work bears the major burden, but a necessary part of which is the provision of a creative discourse.

When such a discourse is lacking, its place is too often taken by catchwords and the type of promotion which belongs rather to the skills of public relations. We have become too used to the dissemination of thoughts and ideas in a "sound-bite" manner which allows for little contemplation and less analysis. The result can be —and many would argue that it must inevitably come to be— a cul-de-sac in which human potential, sensitivity and understanding are trapped and condemned to continually go around in circles. The thirst for truth remains unslaked, and life itself can lose much of its fascination. One senses, however dimly, in a world which offers ready-made solutions on every hand, that the challenge imposed by the intelligent nature of man is not being taken up to the full. But hope is always restored by new vistas, and when a comprehensive system of analysis is proffered, it deserves a heartfelt welcome from the whole body of those who are committed to the ennobling art of literature.

The system of analysis known as semiotics is one such vista. In many ways, it is a culmination of a series of new approaches to literature in the 20th century, especially the various schools of thought which come under the headings of "formalism" and "structuralism". The formalists examined texts in order to discover the progression of a plot through the sequence of its elements, and this linear type of analysis presupposes a syntagmatic pattern. On the other hand, the structuralists examined texts in order to seek out examples of binary oppositions, which reflect basic characteristics of the mind and therefore constitute a paradigmatic pattern. Those who have found much of interest in these approaches to literary analysis, but who consider the one too technical and the other too general, can find in semiotics a system which fulfils the promise of both while rejecting limitations. Having felt some unease at the element of determinism which pervades many systems of analysis, we can rejoice in a consistent system which shows how content and form live in unison and which upholds the independence of the artist as the instigator and creator.

The science of semiotics —and it is surely no exaggeration to describe it as such— is at once concrete in detail and imaginative in range. It derives its power from its roots in human expression, from the continuously great wonder which is human speech and language itself. Born out of words and the urge to communicate, it lauds variety while touching continually on the ultimate source within the human person from which it all springs. As the subject is to the object, and as the living activity of the word is to both, so the progressions in human comprehension call to us as we become aware of the increasing dimensions of life itself. The multidimensionality of creative literature, that one great quality which forever justifies it, is thus made tangible to our very nature, from which and to which it makes its appeal.

Semiotics has long had its appeal for Dr Bronwen Martin, one of the foremost advocates of this system of literary analysis in the English language. When she first explained it to me, I had the mixed feelings of one who senses that here was something of visionary power but which was much too theoretical to encompass all of human experience. I did not then realise that –far from claiming to be an answer to all the questions– the approach of semiotics is rather an invitation to explore. It is a method, or as Dr Martin herself would express it without disparagement, a "tool" which enables one to investigate the how and why of verbal art. It may be any kind of text, but the most important achievement of semiotics is in the context of investigating the narrative scope of literature. It can indeed be claimed that all literature is narrative – not just narrative in the sense of what is described as happening, but narrative in the sense of the total happening. A novel or a story or a poem is in itself an event, and it is a novel or a story or a poem precisely due to the fact that it reveals itself, its various traits relating to each other at ever-deepening levels of consciousness.

By drawing attention to this perennial quality of art, the semiotic method discovers things in the text which the reader never suspected were there, and which, at the subconscious level only, did the writer sense that they were there. In other words, semiotics helps one to gain an appreciation of the wide significance of what is being said.

Appreciation is the apposite term, for all good writers and all good readers feel that the mystery of art can never be fully measured. It is the enduring quality of a creative text that its significance grows ever wider as we investigate it, and somewhere along the line we must stop and be satisfied to enjoy the very fulfilling sense, the stimulation and challenging uncertainty made vivid by aesthetic power.

This book is a clear statement of the principles of semiotics, and it is intended by Dr Martin as an introduction to be used by teachers and by students of literature. Her manner of presentation is direct and easily grasped, and she has chosen by way of illustration a work which is ideally suited for the purpose. This is *Philomel*, a literary parable written in Greek in the year 1943 by Ange S. Vlachos and which has been translated into many languages. Vlachos is a man steeped in literary tradition and is a celebrated novelist and writer of short stories. This is his best-known and most enigmatic work. In recent years it has fascinated a myriad of children, children both young and old, for, as the wise of many traditions have told us, it is the enduring imagination of the child which leaves the adult open to the gaining of wisdom.

Much of Vlachos' writing is concerned with imaginative probing of historical and social situations, and so it is no surprise that his vein of inspiration should dwell for a while on the allegory. In this, he carries on a tradition of incisive search stretching from Plato, through Dante and Bunyan and Swift, to Zamyatin and Orwell in more recent times. The unique atmosphere of *Philomel*, however, derives from its deft use of a genre with universal appeal in popular culture, namely the fable.

Motifs from folklore and mythology, which are readily understood, are set in counterbalance to each other in a manner which fires the imagination and evokes feelings of ever-increasing profundity.

Philomel is a deceptively simple parable, which states less than it suggests and suggests less than it accomplishes. Operating on different levels and resonant with the insight specific to each individual reader, it reaches out into the exciting but ultimately indefinable range of truth. The application of the semiotic method to such a text is in itself a valuable quest and a vivid adventure. In the hands of Dr Martin a whole spectrum of meanings is discovered, and light is shed onto how each meaning is achieved. She goes on to illustrate the relationships between the complex of character, action, and imagery within the text, and invites each reader to probe further into these developing functions.

A reading of Vlachos' story, followed by a study of Martin's technique, and then by a rereading of the story, is indeed an education in the use of words. To travel with both authors is a guarantee of pleasure and enlightenment from creative literature of any kind thereafter.

Dáithí Ó hÓgáin,
University College Dublin

Introduction

The discipline of semiotics is at present enjoying a wave of popularity both in England and abroad: the approach is not only proving increasingly fruitful in the field of literature but also in the wider areas of media studies, of law, medicine and research methods. Nevertheless, in spite of this rising interest, there still remains a reluctance on the part of the general reader to embrace a discipline whose language and terminology is perceived as inherently difficult.

The aim of this book, therefore, is to present as simply as possible the fundamental principles of semiotic analysis at the same time giving a concrete example of their application. I hope thereby to outline a method for textual analysis that will not only be accessible to students of literature but also to all those concerned with language and the production of meaning. The text that has been chosen for analysis is a contemporary Greek fairytale entitled *Philomel: The Forest's Nightingale*[1]. This story was written by the Greek author Ange S. Vlachos in 1943. It was first published in 1993, translated into Irish and English. The wealth of meanings underlying the text together with its exploitation of mythic archetypes make it a particularly fitting vehicle for the introduction of basic semiotic principles.

As readers may be aware, there exist at present many branches of semiotics: the name of Charles Peirce[2], for example, may be familiar to many of us. This book, however, is concerned solely and uniquely with the theories and practice of the Paris School: it is my firm conviction that this school alone can provide the full range of analytical tools necessary for delving beneath the surface of a text.

What is the Paris School?

The Paris School is the name given to a group of researchers that emerged in France in the mid-sixties.

Its founding member is the recently deceased A. J. Greimas. Seminal texts include A. J. Greimas's *Structural Semantics* first published in French in

1966 and the two volumes of *On Meaning* (see bibliography). The theories of this school are also outlined in a dictionary of semiotics produced by its members and practical examples of semiotic analysis appear in their numerous publications. Current participants include D. Bertrand, J. Courtés, J. Fontanille and E. Landowski.

What is Semiotics?

The Paris School defines semiotics as a theory of the production of meaning, that is, a theory describing how meaning is produced. It posits the existence of universal structures, structures which underlie and give rise to meaning. As we shall see, it operates with models that can be applied to any text.

Semiotics takes as its fundamental premise that there can be no meaning without difference. There can be no 'up' without 'down', no 'hot' without 'cold' no 'good' without 'evil'. As Greimas says:

> We perceive differences and thanks to that perception, the world
> 'takes shape' in front of us, and for our purposes[3].

Semiotic analysis, then, is based on four fundamental principles. These are:

1. Meaning is not inherent in objects, objects do not signify by themselves. Meaning, rather, is constructed by what is known as the competent observer ie. by a subject capable of 'giving form' to objects. To give an example, confronted with an implement from a different culture, say African or Asian, we would probably be incapable of grasping its significance. However, left alone with it, we will give it a meaning based on what knowledge we have and on what will suit our purposes.

2. Secondly, semiotics views the text as an autonomous unit, that is, one that is internally coherent. Rather than starting with ideas/meanings external to the text and showing how they are reflected in it, an approach that is still widely adopted in the academic world, semiotic analysis begins with a study of the actual language and structures involved, showing how meanings are constructed (and at the same time, what these meanings are). Semiotic analysis becomes, then, a discovery method and is clearly an invaluable tool for all those engaged in original research.

3. Thirdly, semiotics posits that story-structure or narrativity underlies all discourse, not just what is commonly known as story. For instance, it underlies political, sociological and legal discourse. One can even go as far as to say that narrativity underlies our concept of truth: recent studies in the field of legal discourse, for example, have shown that those witnesses in a law court whose account conforms the most closely to archetypal story patterns are those whose version of events is most likely to be believed.

As we shall be seeing, semiotics makes extensive use of the notion of the *quest* known in metalanguage as the *canonical narrative schema*. The quest highlights the subject/object relationship which is seen as the fundamental structure of the human.

There can be no subject without an object and you do not exist as a human being unless you have a goal. We may note here the influence of phenomenology and of existentialism.

4. Fourthly, semiotics posits the notion of levels of meaning: it is, for instance, the deep abstract level (the thematic level) that generates the surface levels. A text must, therefore, be studied at these different levels of depth and not only at the surface textual level as is the case with traditional linguistics.

I now propose to outline the three levels of meaning known as the figurative level, the narrative level and the deep (or thematic) level: it is this division into levels that constitutes a fundamental procedure in semiotic analysis.

The Figurative Level

The figurative level is a surface level of meaning and the level of the most concrete. All those elements in a text that refer to the external physical world belong to this level: they are known as figures and serve to create the impression of time, place and character. Figurative reality, then, is that reality that can be apprehended by the five senses – vision, smell, hearing, touch and taste. The notations 'forest', 'crawling' 'singing', for instance, are figures. They can be contrasted with the inner world of the conceptual or abstract, that is, with the third and deep level of meaning.

The figurative level clearly plays a very important part in literature. It is, however, equally important in the construction of news stories: the journalist seeks to present an event as vividly as possible: like the novelist, s/he is aiming at producing a reality effect.

The Narrative Level

The narrative level is more general and more abstract than the figurative level: it is the level of story-structure, a structure that, as we have said, underlies all discourse. In our analysis of this level, we apply two fundamental narrative models that were first elaborated by A. J. Greimas. These are **a**) the actantial narrative schema **b**) the canonical narrative schema (see Chapter One).

The Deep Level

Known also as the thematic level, the deep level is the level of the abstract or conceptual: it relates to the inner mental world as opposed to the outer physical world of the figurative level. Concepts such as those of 'good' and 'evil', 'justice' and 'injustice' belong to this level. It is the level at which are articulated the fundamental values of a text.

This division into levels provides the fundamental structure for this book. The first chapter is devoted to an examination of the narrative level, the second to the figurative and the third to the deep level. I have chosen to begin with the narrative level in order to introduce the reader to a number of key concepts of semiotics necessary for the understanding of the book. Once these concepts have been grasped, I suggest that ideally a semiotic analysis of a text should begin with a study of the figurative level and then procede to an examination of the narrative level and finally to that of the deep level. In other words, the direction is from surface to depth and the process is one of decoding.

Throughout the book the principles of semiotics are illustrated through a close reading of the story of *Philomel*. I hope in the process to have awakened the reader's interest in this fable and to have encouraged her/him to pursue the quest to unravel its tapestry of meanings.

Notes to Introduction

1. Ange S. Vlachos is the author of numerous novels and essays (see biographical notes, pp. 96-97)

2. Charles Peirce (1839-1914). Peirce's philosophy has exerted a strong influence in the U.S.A. This branch of semiotics is concerned above all with questions of epistemology and of logic

3. *Sémantique structurale,* Paris, Larousse, 1966, p. 19

Philomel
The Forest's Nightingale

"Hush!... Hush!... All of you! Have a little rest now or else you will not hear your father singing."

"Will father sing tonight?"

"Yes he will and the Moon will rise to listen to him. Philomel! Fold your wings! Make room for your brothers!"

"But... I am too big! What can I do? There isn't room for four..."

"Be quiet! Don't forget that you were hatched last! Well, this evening when it is dark, your father will start singing. You must keep quiet. The night will come when you will sing and the Moon will rise to listen..."

"What is the Moon, mother?"

"The Moon is... oh, well, you'll see the Moon tonight. Hush now, the day is ending, sleep a little. Come closer all of you, closer, under here my children, rest now."

Donna covered her little nightingales with her wings and began a lullaby. Her voice is not as beautiful as her husband's and she knows it. So she sings only for her children.

And now she is preoccupied with them and disregards the slight crackle. Such a slight crackle like a shrivelled leaf when, stirred by the sigh of the breeze, it rustles over its dead brothers.

A stealthy, creeping sound on the trunk of the linden tree.

"Rest eh!" Chea hissed, "rest for your children! I have a bone to pick with you woman! You're so boastful! You say the Moon rises at your husband's bidding to listen to his chatter all night long!

The Moon rises for me! It is for me it wanders, lingering all night! The Moon is looking for me from the sky! But you... You can not know that!"

Chea uttered her soliloquy, undulating and creeping higher up the tree. She pauses now and then, darting her little head this way, that way.

Like two little pins, her two small eyes penetrate every shadow around her, searching in case someone from the world above, the world of the birds, might see her and alert Donna. There is also the fear of old Vigo, the Night's Sentinel.

"Hum, him! I must strike him in the daytime. The accursed one! I must root him out and exterminate him with my bite. In the daytime! He cannot see then! So tremble my sweet Donna! I will swallow and devour all the birds of the Forest!"

Chea is a long and dark snake and has a pair of hollow poisonous fangs in her mouth. Night-time or not, her eyes always look menacing. The birds, the mice, the weasels, even her cousins —the tree-snakes and the water-snakes— avoid her eyes. All the animals know that if you look into her eyes, reason takes flight and madness overcomes you.

Chea the Lithe, possesses this power from bygone days, since the days when fairies and goblins used to play in the glades of the Forest by the light of the Moon.

In those days Chea was the daughter of a King, a daughter of fascinating beauty who wore a crown.

Even now, as a snake, Chea has a circlet on her little head and she boasts that there her crown used to sit. She maintains that once her mouth is freed of these poisonous fangs, she will regain her long-lost crown.

So in those days Chea used to go dancing, with the other maidens, by the light of the Moon.

And one night, the kind of night that entrances the world and its creatures, when the flowers —narcissuses, crocuses and hyacinths— bewildered stay awake, when even the butterflies do not sleep but fly from blossom to blossom communicating, in the gentlest of whispers, their deepest secrets, on a night like this, when the Forest holds its breath to listen to the song of the Nightingale and, beyond the distant hills, the Moon rises in the sky: Chea revelled in her dance, tiptoeing on the grass and the flowers, and the Son of Faie saw her for the first time and... lost his head! He had looked into her eyes and... reason took flight and madness overcame him !

From that moment on, the Son of Faie could think of nothing except to capture Chea. A bush became his hiding place and one night he leapt out and grabbed her.

The frightened maidens, fairies and goblins flew away from the glades into the woods and Chea was left alone with him. Next came their wedding and the entire Forest celebrated for a month.

I think it was either April or May when Chea and the Son of Faie were married. And as everybody partook in merriment and joy forgetting evil thoughts or deeds, the Night's Sentinel had nothing to guard. Vigo was off duty for the whole month !

Down in the Marshes, amongst the reeds, the Frogs have their Kingdom. They croak all night defending it from the other animals.
Defend what ! Muddy waters and rotten leaves !
Oh well ! It is their Kingdom.

Down in these Marshes, there lived an Ogre, they say, but actually what they say is Runa's gossiping, Runa, the Magpie who sits idle, tittle-tattling, all day long. Anyway, they say that this Ogre had a treasure hidden amongst the reeds of the Marshes and, according to these rumours, the Ogre emerged, one day, from the mire, went to the spring, beside the large sycamore, washed and spruced himself and entered the Forest. There the Ogre found Chea surrounded by her bees; they were teaching her the art of making blossom honey.

That day Chea's husband was far away, he had gone to see his mother, the witch Faie. The sight of the Ogre terrified Chea. She had never seen a stranger in the Forest before and the Ogre was so ugly! A real monster! The Ogre talked to Chea in a gentle voice. He told her all about his riches and his jewels and if she would come, he said, into the Marshes, to the Kingdom of the Frogs, he would unearth all his treasures and offer them to her : "I cannot, I cannot leave the Forest," said Chea "I must never leave the Forest!"

"Can you imagine how many jewels, how many precious stones I have in the Marshes! It is worth just taking a look at them", the Ogre insisted. And from that day on, the Ogre often went to see Chea and, every time, he promised her his treasures, if she would only leave the Forest and go with him to the Marshes.

And, one day, as her husband, exhausted from the heat, lay sleeping, Chea left the Forest and went to the Marshes.

As she was about to enter, the wind blew and the reeds around her whispered:

"Where are you going Chea? Where are you going? Go back!"

But the Frogs, who had received their instructions from the Ogre, started to croak: "Here comes the Queen! She has arrived. The Queen has arrived!" And Chea entered.

When her husband awoke, he started searching for her.

He asked the birds, he questioned the flowers but no one had anything to tell him. From high above, Nisoos the hawk, who hovers all day between sky and earth and sees everything that happens in the world, called to him:

" To the Marshes ! Go to the Marshes ! "

He ran to the Marshes and saw Chea emerging from the muddy waters, filthy from the mire. In the depths, amongst the reeds, he also saw the Ogre who was laughing at him. Trembling with rage, the Son of Faie, in his fury, called his mother, the Witch.

Faie bound Chea's feet, threw her to the ground, snatched her crown, put poison in her mouth and cast a fearful spell on her:

"From now on, filthy as when you emerged from the
mire, you will crawl on your belly and whatever you
eat from your mouth will be poisoned."

Chea, rolling on the ground, begged for mercy and Faie, who did not wish to deprive any creature on earth of all hope, told her that only if she killed a bird while it is singing, could she be released from her curse. The poison would then be discharged from her mouth, she would become the King's daughter once again, and rise high into the sky to seek her husband.

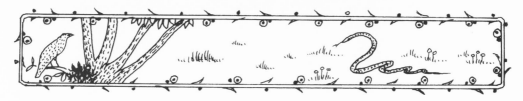

Since those far-off days the King's daughter has become a snake. Creeping on her belly, she bites everyone who crosses her path, hoping to get rid of the venom from her fangs but, in vain. And Chea's days are filled with despair.

ΑΓΓΕΛΟΣ ΒΛΑΧΟΣ

ΕΙΚΟΝΕΣ :—

ΠΑΥΛΟΣ ΒΛΑΧΟΣ

ΑΘΗΝΑ 1947

So, creeping up the linden tree, she stopped and her little eyes penetrated the shadows. She could hear Donna restlessly moving in her nest as if she were frightened by the absolute silence which suddenly falls upon the Forest at this hour. The twilight hour, when the activities and movements of the Day stop and the mysteries of the Night begin. At this hour even Chea would crawl lazily in the grass looking for a cool place to spend the night. But this evening, she is out for prey and she must hurry along. In no time, he will come back, he, the conceited one who sings all night believing that the entire Forest, together with the Moon, listens to him! If he should return to his nest, then Chea would have to fight with two birds. And two birds who fight for their children are a peck of trouble, even for Chea.

She crept up, curled her body and fixed her eyes on the nest. At that very moment, a faint whistle was heard, so faint, only a snake's ears could detect it: "Vigo! The Night's Sentinel! Already awake?" And Chea slithered down into the darkness.

The Night's Sentinel is the only bird in the Forest who can see through the darkness.

The stars had come out one by one. The larger ones first, in accordance with the order of the sky, then all the others.

Down below, in the Forest, the Fireflies started to stir. They used to be stars once, the Fireflies say, that fell to earth. In spring they shimmer and fly from bush to bush. They assume the time will come for them to ascend, once again, to where they belong, high in the sky. They say one night without malice in the Forest would suffice, then they would rise high...

Suddenly, in the profound silence of the Forest, the song of the Nightingale was heard. The wild violets who whisper when the light of the day ends and every fragrant whisper from them perfumes the air, yearned for the song in the half light; the little owl who every now and then stops his solitary chatter and pricks up an ear, longed to hear it; even the silent stream which flows so calmly as if it has stopped, craved for the song to begin. And higher than the trees escalated the voice of the Nightingale, scale by scale it was raised to be heard in the heavens. And as the entire Forest listened to the song which floated with the Night, little by little, beyond the distant hills, rose the Moon.

"The Nightingale has lost its reason! He is mad!" the little owl was crying. And the wild violets, low in the grass, whispered :

"If only the same could happen to us..."

To learn how to fly is not an easy task even if you are a bird.

Donna returned, one day, to her nest and found her sons jumping about and flapping their wings. The time had arrived for them to fly. And soon Vigo would come to teach them about the world.

One afternoon, when the sun sits in the middle of the sky and all living creatures, exhausted from the heat, look for shade, Donna placed Philomel on the rim of the nest and told him to look down at Zeena, the may-beetle, who was buzzing in a patch of light like those the sun makes through the leaves. Zeena was playing with the light and the light with her and Philomel craned further and further to take a closer look at their game.

It was then that Donna nudged him gently out of the nest and, it happened: Philomel stretched out his wings and slowly glided to the ground, close to the place where Zeena was playing. Donna flew after him to protect him.

Philomel, adventurous, felt immense joy at the abundance of space and started to strut about. He began to flap his wings and to chirp noisily with delight.

Donna, worried the noise might awaken an enemy, scolded Philomel to quieten him down but Philomel would not comply. A voice was heard from above, saying:

"I have never seen such a brave little nightingale before !"

Philomel raised his head to see who was talking. It was Lady Squirrel who, high up, on a bough, was looking at him with deceitful eyes.

Lady Squirrel is a peculiar animal. While she is chewing a hazel-nut or something similar, she sits on her hind legs, joins her front little paws, thanking the Lord who feeds her.

Hypocrisy, no doubt! She is the only one who claims to be praying and the only one who believes it!

Donna was startled at Lady Squirrel's voice. This crafty Lady, who jumps from bough to bough as if she has a spring inside her and she has four legs —did you hear? four!— this lady, when playing, sometimes gives scratches that can kill!

"Bless the little Nightingale! Bless you! You've sent him into the world too soon, Madame," said Lady Squirrel and started to come down from the boughs to the trunk and from the trunk to reach the ground at such speed that Philomel had scarcely time to fly onto a low branch and from there to another one higher until he arrived at his nest. From there he shouted at the top of his voice :
"You are a wicked animal!" Philomel caused the utmost confusion to his slumbering brothers: "What on earth is going on? What is the matter with you, Philomel?"
"I came across Danger!"
"What is that? Danger? What does it look like?" All his brothers wanted to know. And as a true expert. Philomel announced :
"Danger has four legs !"
"Four legs! How's that?"
"Danger has many legs," said mother Donna, "so many, they cannot be counted."

So Philomel had started to learn about the ways of the world. For other, more serious, matters, Vigo came to teach him. Vigo explained briefly to Philomel the constitution of the Forest. Philomel learned that in the Forest exist two worlds: the one below and the one above. He learned that the first tries constantly to do its utmost to harm the second. He also learned that the weasels, martens, foxes and ferrets as well as all the other creatures that run and jump in the world below, apart from the Hare, constitute a living Danger.

Vigo gave him advice on nutrition: grasshoppers, spiders and insects of all kinds promote growth, he said, but he warned Philomel never to pick up filthy worms. They come from a lower world, a muddy and dirty one. They are distant relatives of Chea, the frightful snake...

And at this point, Philomel's mind began to wander. He was trying to imagine that peculiar creature and how you could lose your reason by looking into her eyes.

"Has Chea beautiful eyes?" asked Philomel.

"No! No! They are dull and evil, all creatures have clear eyes, only hers...", said the wise old Bird and shuddered as if he had remembered something from the days of his youth...

"And has she no mercy for anyone?"

"Mercy? One must have a heart to have mercy. Chea has no heart since the day she was cursed. Sometimes though, when your father sings in the night, she lingers, wandering like the Moon. Something from her past, when she used to dance with the fairies, must remain in her."

"Vigo, do you remember Chea when she was the King's daughter?"

"It is a very old story. My grandfather, to whom the story was told by his grandfather who had heard it from others, recounted it to me!"

"And will she ever be the King's daughter again?"

"They say she will regain her crown only if she kills a Luscinia while it is singing."

"A Luscinia? What is a Luscinia, Vigo?"

"A bird, a songbird... Killing a songbird while it is singing! That's impossible!"

Vigo flew back to his lofty abode and left Philomel alone. Philomel remained on the branch of the linden tree and searched for Chea over the floor of the world below. He recalled Vigo's words:

"Never look into her eyes, never!"

But Philomel had to see her. He wanted to see what she looked like... this daughter of a King.

The Days passed and the Nights followed, changing nothing in the Forest, except that Philomel, nightingale that he was, had taught himself how to sing. His voice was so sweet and he could sing such beautiful songs, that even the crickets ceased their unendurable nocturnal chatter to listen to him.

The more Philomel grew and the more he sang, the more confident he became and he started flying closer to the world below the trees, into low-spreading branches and bushes, observing every kind of activity.

The ants became his friends, he never harmed them. They used to stop in their path to talk to him about their hard work, to explain how heavily laden they were all day long and how tired they became by the end of the day.

They wondered why Philomel had condescended to listen to them. So they advised him to be vigilant because, in the world below the high trees, over the floor of the Forest, there are many vicious enemies. Only the Hare harms no one.

Philomel flew in search of the Hare. He found him nibbling and chewing. He was moving his lips up and down as if the tender, bursting shoots disgusted him.

The Hare heard the flapping of Philomel's wings and flattened his long ears back, crouching on the ground.

"Don't be scared!" called Philomel and landed on a branch nearby.

"Oh! It's you!" sighed the Hare with relief, "you frightened me out of my wits!"

"Do Hares have wits?" Philomel teased him.

"I am a docile, humble animal", said the Hare. "I do not harm anybody."

"I know that! Vigo and the ants told me! So, what's it like to live down here?"

"To live here? We live with fear in our hearts and we lose heart from fear."

"Are you all afraid?"

"Of course we are! Didn't you know that? The marten is afraid of the weasel, the weasel is afraid of the ferret, the ferret is afraid of the fox and the fox is afraid of the wolf. Everyone is trained by fear down here and everybody dreads Chea. As for myself, I fear them all, including Chea - and my shadow."

"You're so harebrained and such a coward!" cried Philomel and flew away. But, by now, Philomel had learned about the circle of fear that binds all creatures to the same fate.

The Days were passing by and, along with them, Summer. It was nearing the time when trees, tired of holding their leaves, slowly begin to shed them onto the ground, yellow and faded.

Autumn was approaching.

One morning, Donna heard a honking noise from the sky. She looked through the canopy of the linden tree. High up, in the azure of the sky, she saw the familiar V-shape: the geese!

"We must get ready!" she said and started giving instructions to Philomel and his brothers, preparing them for the long journey they were about to take.

And it was at that crucial moment that Philomel said to his mother that he wanted to see Chea. Donna's heart leapt into her mouth!

"Have you taken leave of your senses Philomel? You have grown up and become a real nightingale, but where are your brains? Imagine wanting to see Chea! You've lost your mind before even seeing her!"

"Mother, if I meet Chea and sing to her, she might get rid of the poison in her mouth and become the King's daughter once again. And so the world below us will be freed from her evil."

"Philomel! Get it out of your mind! What does the world below us matter to you?"

Philomel flew away to seek advice from Vigo. The sun had not yet set and Vigo was still asleep.

Philomel sat on a branch nearby to wait and then: he saw close, very close to Vigo's tree a long dark creature. It stirred and undulated on the ground. "It is Chea, the bewitched daughter! She is crawling on her belly. She is going to bite Vigo! But it is not yet dark and he cannot see! He cannot even move!" Philomel flew closer and called out: "Vigo, be careful, Vigo! Chea is heading for your tree!"

Vigo heard him but did not move. Philomel began fluttering round Chea. Chea forgot Vigo and turned to Philomel.
"Look at me, you little idiot!
Look into my eyes and stop singing! You are annoying me!"

But Philomel knew everything and avoided her eyes.
Still singing, he took flight – with Chea in pursuit.
Vigo was left alone. From his tree-abode he hearkened to the sound of Philomel's wings and Chea's hissing.

Deep silence. Stillness in the Forest. There was only Vigo, impatient and anxious for the sun to set. And as the light dimmed, he flew in the same direction he had last heard Philomel and Chea.

Not far from there, on the ground, with wings outstretched, Philomel lay lifeless and... next to him...

"What is it ? What is this strange thing ?" thought Vigo.

Around Philomel, hosts of his friends, the ants, had gathered. They had heard the bad news and had hurried there to see. Vigo wept for Philomel and then he looked all around him.

"Where on earth is Chea ?" he wondered.

In the first shadows of the Night, the Fireflies provided the answer. "At last we will rise into the sky! High up above, where Chea has gone," they called to one another. The Night's Sentinel turned his head to the sky and saw between the Little and the Great Bear a line of shining stars which resembled the shape of Chea. He saw her long body which winds around like a serpent amongst the other stars and her little head with the two glittering eyes.

Amazed, Vigo lowered his head. He looked down to the ground: Philomel lay lifeless and next to him the cast-off skin of Chea !

Not even a sigh was heard in the Forest.
Serenity reigned high in the trees and higher in the sky.
Peace had nestled in the world below.

Ange S. Vlachos

Chapter One

The Narrative Level

Narrative structure has always been a central concern of the Paris School of Semiotics: indeed it was from an analysis of the narrative archetypes of fairy tale and myth that the school was born.

The first chapter of this study, therefore, will be devoted to an examination of what is known as the narrative level of meaning.

What is the narrative level?

The narrative level of meaning can be described as the level of story-grammar, that is, the level at which operate universal syntactic structures of meaning. Let us begin, therefore, by addressing a key question:

How do we recognise a story or narrative?
What are its essential features?

I would like to propose the following definition of a story:

1. Firstly, a narrative presents an event: something happens or, to be precise, there is a change of state or movement from one state of affairs to another. A bank robbery is an event because we move from an initial state –the presence of the money– to a final state –the absence of the money. A purely descriptive passage, on the other hand, does not present an event: the state of affairs at the end of the text is the same as at the beginning. In semiotic terminology, the expression *narrative programme* may also be used to designate an event.

If we look at the global story of *Philomel,* what happens is that the nightingale, Philomel, is killed by the snake, Chea. The snake is thereby released from her curse and peace descends on the Forest. A change of state has clearly taken place: Philomel moves from an initial state of being alive to a final state of being dead.

Philomel:

$$s \longrightarrow s^1$$

life   death

At the same time, the Forest moves from a state of conflict to one of harmony:

Forest:

$$s \longrightarrow s^1$$

conflict   harmony

2. Secondly, the movement from one state to another is always expressed in terms of an *opposition*. The story of Cinderella moves from poor to rich and from a state of humiliation to one of elevation. In adverts for soap powder, the initial state is that of being dirty and the final state that of being clean. A story that progressed from a state of poverty to one of good health would not make sense.

Two terms are deemed to be in opposition (known as contraries) if they possess at least one feature in common. 'Up' and 'down' have verticality in common: we say that 'up' and 'down' articulate the semantic category of verticality or that they are two poles on the semantic axis of verticality:

Semantic axis (category) of verticality

up   **vs**   down

where **vs** indicates opposition.

'Black' and 'white' have colour in common: they articulate the semantic category of colour or represent the two poles on the semantic axis of colour:

Semantic axis of colour

black   **vs**   white

The change of state that we examined in *Philomel* can now be presented in terms of the following oppositions:

Semantic axis: **state of existence**

life   **vs**   death

Semantic axis: **moral state**

conflict   **vs**   harmony

3. Thirdly, a change of state –the movement from one pole of the semantic axis to its opposite– always implies an act of *transformation*. A story unfolds in time, it has direction, there is always a 'before' and an 'after':

$$\mathbf{s} \text{———————} \mathbf{T} \text{————→} \mathbf{s^1}$$

where **T** indicates a transformation.

Sometimes the initial or the final state is not manifested (explicit) in the text but simply implied. In this case, to make sense, the reader must resort to an underlying logic. When an advert shows us a clean garment produced by a particular soap powder, we assume, of course, that it was originally dirty.

A story, then is always organised with its end in mind: it is the final situation or state that determines the chain of preceding events:

before	transformation	after
s	**T**	**s¹**
initial state		final state
reversal of final state		outcome of event

It is, for example, because the money is gone (**s¹**-outcome of event) that I am relating the theft of the money (transformation) which was originally in the bank (**s**-reversal of final state or outcome).

The two principal transformations in *Philomel* are:

a) The snake Chea attacks and kills Philomel. Unusual for a fairy story, this transformation is not manifested in the text: the reader deduces what has happened from the statement 'with wings outstretched, Philomel lay lifeless' (p. 31) :

before	transformation	after
Philomel alive	Philomel attacked by Chea	Philomel dead

b) Chea, released from her curse, leaves the earth (and her snakeskin) and goes up into the sky where she appears as a line of stars. Again, the transformation is not manifested: it is the Fireflies who let us know what has happened: 'At last we will rise into the sky! High up above, where Chea has gone' (p. 31):

before	transformation	after
Chea on earth as snake	Chea leaves earth	Chea in sky as a line of stars

Transformations can be sudden or progressive. The two examples from the story of *Philomel* —the nightingale's death and the snake's ascent to the sky— are sudden. A progressive transformation is one in which there is an element of hesitation, where the possibility of an alternative outcome to the situation remains very real. A classic example of this, frequently quoted by semioticians, is the passage describing the taming of the lion in J. Kessel's 'Le Lion'[1].

How do we begin our analysis ?

A semiotic analysis of the narrative begins, then, with an examination of the global structure of the text. In order to do this, the following procedure must be adopted:

1. Begin your analysis by looking at the end of the text (or passage). Can you ascertain what is the final state of affairs or situation? It is only by looking first at this final state that we know which traits are relevant to describe the initial state: the latter is not necessarily defined in the first line, first paragraph or even the first chapter of a novel.

2. Now find the corresponding initial state. The relationship between the two (beginning and end) must be one of opposition.

In the story of *Philomel*, the final state is that harmony reigns in the Forest. This is presented explicitly in the following utterances —known as *utterances of state:*

> Not even a sigh was heard in the Forest. Serenity reigned high
> in the trees and higher in the sky.
> Peace had nestled in the world below (p. 31).

The initial state must, then, be the reversal of this final state – it must be one of conflict. Conflict is indeed suggested in the opening paragraphs in the description of the snake Chea (pp. 17, 18) and in her soliloquy (pp. 17-18). The snake is clearly a threat to all the birds of the Forest:

> So tremble my sweet Donna !
> I will swallow and devour all the birds of the Forest ! (p.18).

This state of affairs remains static until just before the end of the story when the transformation occurs.

3. Having found the underlying opposition, look for the principle transformation(s) in the text. As we have seen, the two main transformations –the killing of Philomel and Chea's ascent into the sky– are implied in the story and take place shortly before its close (p. 31).

4. Finally, state whether the transformation is sudden or progressive.

Both opposition and transformation are, then, fundamental features of narrative. There are few texts, however, that contain only one (or indeed two) transformations: most texts contain several, each one being termed an *episode*. Before proceeding with your analysis, therefore, you may wish to divide your text into episodes. If your passage is lengthy, you may select only those episodes that appear of greater significance.

Episodes

An episode is the name we give to a fragment of a text that constitutes a story in itself. In other words, an episode must contain a transformation and this transformation must form an integral part of a global narrative or story. The structure is therefore hierarchical and may be similar to that of Chinese boxes.

If we look at the narrative trajectory of the bird, Philomel, the following pattern emerges: the list of episodes is not necessarily exhaustive:

Philomel

Global Transformation:
Philomel is killed: his story moves from life to death (from **s** to **s¹**).

Episodes (transformations within this global one)

A. Philomel learns to fly and leaves his nest (p. 25).
B. Philomel meets Lady Squirrel: his first encounter with danger (pp. 25, 26).
C. Philomel's encounter with the owl, Vigo: he acquires knowledge of Chea and of evil (pp. 27-28).
D. Philomel's encounter with the hare: he learns about the circle of fear (p. 29).
E. Philomel's visit to Vigo, intending to ask his advice. Instead he meets Chea and sings to her (p. 30).

Diagram:

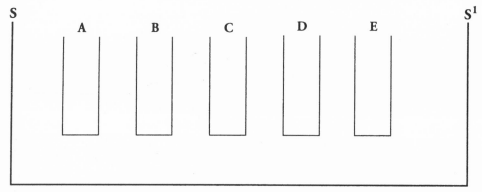

Each of these episodes can be seen as a *sub* or *use narrative programme* within a *global narrative programme* - the movement from life to death.

If we look at the narrative trajectory of the snake, Chea, the following pattern emerges:

Chea

Global Transformation

Chea ascends into heaven and becomes a line of stars. Her story has therefore moved from snake to star ($s \longrightarrow s^1$).

Episodes

Chea's narrative path includes the following episodes:

A. Chea crawls up the tree in pursuit of the nightingale (pp. 17, 18, 23).
B. Chea goes to attack Vigo (p. 31)
C. Chea pursues Philomel and kills him (p. 31).

The structure is presented in the diagram below:

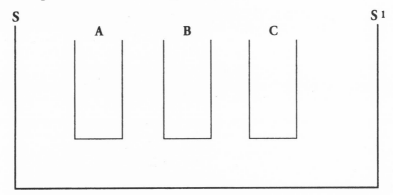

The semiotic analysis of a text does not always require its division into episodes. However, this procedure can sometimes help us to elicit and clarify the underlying structure and to locate the key narrative programmes. When confronted with a very long text, the reader may also wish to focus the analysis on one or two episodes.

Having presented a general outline of narrative structure, I would now like to draw attention to two fundamental narrative models that, according to the Paris School, operate within every text. These models were elaborated by A. J. Greimas in the sixties; they are known as **a)** *the actantial schema* **b)** *the canonical narrative schema*. The next stage of our analysis, then, will be to apply these schemas.

The Actantial Schema

When V. Propp analysed the Russian folktale, he found 31 narrative functions that were common to all of these texts, functions such as those of hero, donor, traitor and villain. Greimas reduces the number of these functions to six, thus producing a more workable model.[2] These are:

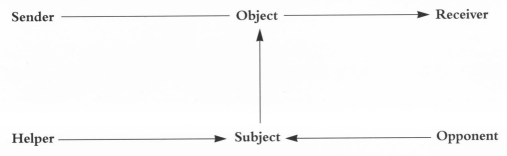

Together these six actants and their organization account for all possible relationships within a story and indeed within the sphere of human action in general. As we shall see, these narrative positions –known also as actantial roles– may be held by people, places, objects or abstract ideas.

The actantial roles are distributed on three axes:

1. The axis of desire: subject and object.
2. The axis of power: helper and opponent.
3. The axis of communication: sender and receiver.

Let us begin by examining the axis of desire.

The Axis of Desire.

The narrative trajectory from the initial situation to the final situation in a story takes the form of a *quest*: a subject goes in pursuit of an object. But what exactly do we mean by the terms subject and object?

I would like to propose the following definitions:

The Subject

In a story the position of subject may be held by any actor (character) who performs an action. The subject is always in pursuit of an object or goal. The two positions are considered inseparable: in other words, you cannot be a true subject or real human being unless you have an object or goal.

In *Philomel* the two principal actors, the nightingale Philomel and the snake Chea, are both subjects of a quest. Philomel's aim, for example, is to sing to Chea and release her from her curse thus freeing the world of evil (p. 30). Chea is likewise in pursuit of a goal: her aim is to kill a bird while it is singing thus releasing herself from the curse and becoming the King's daughter once again (pp. 18, 21).

Very often this quest is motivated by a deficiency or a *lack*, that is, by an awareness of a missing object. Indeed, this sense of loss has been considered by some to be the wellspring of all human action and hence of all stories.

To be more precise, we can now say that at the beginning of a story the subject is frequently presented as disjoined from the object.

The relationship can be expressed thus:

$$S \cup O$$

where $\cup$ indicates disjunction.

At the end, if the subject is successful, it is said to be conjoined with the object:

$$S \cap O$$

where $\cap$ indicates conjunction.

Sometimes, of course, the reverse process takes place : the subject moves from conjunction to disjunction. A classic example of this would be A. Daudet's story *The Fable of the Man with the Golden Brain* where one of the principal quests is to preserve the gold.

In *Philomel* the two subjects, Philomel and Chea, are initially disjoined from their objects :

Philomel: $S \cup O$

Philomel   singing to Chea, freeing Forest from curse of evil

Chea: $S \cup O$

Chea   killing a bird whilst it is singing, releasing herself from curse

At the end of the story, both subjects succeed in their quest, they are, therefore, said to be conjoined with their object: Philomel sings to Chea (pp. 30, 31), Chea kills him whilst he is singing (p. 31) and ascends to the sky.

This fundamental change between subject and object —the movement towards conjunction or disjunction— describes what is known as a *narrative programme*. The states of disjunction/conjunction mark the beginning and end of such a programme.

It is at this point in our analysis that a distinction must be made between two different kinds of subject: *a subject of state* (known also as a subject of being) and *a subject of doing*. Let us once more define our terms.

Subject of state

A subject of state is a subject that is essentially static. It is qualified by verbs such as 'to be' or 'to have' (including their negative forms). For example: 'he is sad', 'we are not amused' and 'I have no money'. We call the above sentences *utterances of state* and they constitute what is traditionally known as description.

Examples of this type of utterance in *Philomel* are :

> Chea is a long and dark snake and has a pair of hollow poisonous fangs in her mouth (p. 18).
> They (Chea's eyes) are dull and evil, all creatures have clear eyes (p. 27).
> Chea has no heart (p. 27).
> The marten is afraid of the weasel, the weasel is afraid of the ferret (p. 29).

There are two types of utterances of state:

a) *Conjunctive utterances of state:*

This means that the subject is conjoined with the object :

$$S \quad \cap \quad O$$

and she has a pair of hollow poisonous fangs (p. 18)

b) *Disjunctive utterances of state :*

This means that the subject is disjoined with the object :

$$S \quad \cup \quad O$$

Chea has no heart (p. 27)

The subject of state may be contrasted with the subject of doing.

Subject of doing

The subject of doing is essentially dynamic. It is qualified by 'doing' verbs: 'she went to Spain', 'he bought a book'.

The above sentences or clauses are known as utterances of doing. Examples in our chosen text are:

> She (Chea) crept up, curled her body and fixed her eyes on the nest (p. 23).
> And Lady Squirrel started to come down from the boughs to the trunk (p. 26).
> Philomel flew in search of the Hare (p. 29).

44

Utterances of doing present the change from one utterance of state to its opposite, that is, from a state of disjunction to conjunction or vice versa.

As we have already seen, in order for the subject of state –designated here as S^2– who is initially disjoined from the object $(S^2 \cup O)$ to be eventually conjoined with it $(S^2 \cap O)$ there must be a transformation or a transforming doing –frequently indicated by a capital F. This transformation is carried out by a subject of doing, presented here as S^1.

The subject of doing (S^1) can be the same actor as the subject of state (S^2): 'I (S^2) am hungry and I (S^1) get something to eat'.

This pattern is expressed in the following equation :

$$F \ [\ S^1 \ \text{..............} > (S^2 \quad \cap \quad O) \ ]$$

The action is known as a *reflexive doing*: S^2 and S^1 are the same actors. The structure is one of *acquisition*.

In *Philomel* the episode describing the marriage of the Son of Faie to the King's daughter, Chea, can be presented in a similar manner:

$$\begin{array}{ccccc} F & [\ S^1 & \text{..............} > (S^2 & \cap & O) \ ] \\ \text{marriage} & \text{Son} & \text{Son} & & \text{Chea} \\ & \text{of Faie} & \text{of Faie} & & \end{array}$$

The subject of doing (S^1) can, of course, be a different actor from the subject of state (S^2): 'I (S^2) am hungry and someone (S^1) gives me something to eat'.

The equation would look similar to the above except the S^1 and S^2 are represented by different actors. This action is known as a *transitive doing* and the structure is that of the gift. The episode where Vigo imparts his knowledge to Philomel could take the following form :

$$\begin{array}{ccccc} F & [\ S^1 & \text{..............} > (S^2 & \cap & O) \ ] \\ \text{giving} & \text{Vigo} & \text{Philomel} & & \text{knowledge} \end{array}$$

Here the position of S^1 and S^2 are clearly held by different actors.

In the analysis of the story of *Philomel*, my primary concern will be the narrative programme of the quest. I shall be concentrating, therefore, on those instances where the subject of doing and the subject of state coincide. Let us now go on to examine a second key actantial role, that of the object.

The Object

There can be no subject in a narrative without there being at the same time an object. In other words, the action of a subject must be orientated towards a goal. In R.L. Stevenson's *Treasure Island*, the subject of the quest is Jim Hawkins and its object the treasure.

The subject, then, goes in search of an object. The role of object could be held by:

1. A human being, zoomorphic or anthropomorphic agent.
   In a detective story, the detective (subject) could be looking for the guilty person (object).

2. A material element.
   In an adventure story, the hero (subject) could be seeking treasure (object).

3. An abstract idea or an emotion.
   In a psychological novel or Bildungsroman, the subject may be on a quest for knowledge of the world (object) or maturity (object).

In the case of numbers **1** and **2** above the object is *pragmatic*, that is, we are in the realm of the concrete and the physical. In the case of number **3**, however, we are concerned with the inner conceptual world of thought and feeling and with abstract values such as those of knowledge and truth. The object of the quest is, therefore, *cognitive*.

In the course of a story, an actor may have more than one quest. The initial goal of Philomel's actions is to acquire knowledge of the world and to satisfy his curiosity (p. 17). This is conveyed in his first utterance:

What is the Moon, mother ? (p. 17)

It also explains his subsequent meetings with Lady Squirrel (pp. 25-26), with Vigo (pp. 27-28), with the Hare (p. 29) and with the ants:

He started flying closer to the world below the trees, into low-spreading branches and bushes, observing every kind of activity (p. 28).

Later, when the nightingales are about to undertake their journey South, Philomel expresses the desire to sing to Chea, thus freeing the Forest from her curse. This now becomes his main quest:

> Mother, if I meet Chea and sing to her, she might get rid of the poison
> in her mouth and become the King's daughter once again. And so the
> world below us will be freed from her evil (p. 30).

His first quest, the pursuit of knowledge, can thus be considered a subsidiary or use narrative programme ie. one that helps him carry out his principal programme.

I shall now go on to consider a second set of actantial roles, that is, the positions of *helper* and *opponent* situated on the axis of power.

The Axis of Power

The Helper

Any actor who helps the subject in its quest is known as a helper. A subject may have one or more helpers; again this role may be held by people, animals, objects or abstract concepts including the emotions.

In the fairytale, *Cinderella*, the fairy-godmother and the coach function as helpers in Cinderella's quest to go to the ball.

In his initial quest for knowledge, the nightingale, Philomel, has several helpers:

1. His mother Donna who helps him to fly:

> Donna placed Philomel on the rim of the nest and told him to look
> down at Zeena, the maybeetle (p.25)
> It was then that Donna nudged him gently out of the nest and, it
> happened (p. 25).

2. The owl Vigo who teaches him about the Forest and about conflict and danger:

> Vigo explained briefly to Philomel the constitution of the Forest.
> Philomel learned that in the Forest exist two worlds: the one below and
> the one above. He learned that the first tries constantly to do its utmost
> to harm the second (p. 27).

Vigo also provides him with invaluable information about the snake, Chea. He tells him about her curse, for example, and about the evil she spreads (pp. 27-28).

3. The ants who also warn Philomel about the dangers of the Forest:
> So they advised him to be vigilant because, in the world below the high trees, over the floor of the Forest, there are many vicious enemies (p. 29).

4. Philomel's own bravery and adventurous spirit are also helpers (pp. 26, 28):
> Philomel, adventurous, felt immense joy at the abundance of space (p. 25).

Lady Squirrel comments:
> I have never seen such a brave little nightingale before (p. 26).

Chea, the snake, likewise has her helpers in her quest to kill a bird while it is singing although they are much fewer in number. Daylight, for example, may be considered her primary helper: Vigo, the Night's Sentinel, is asleep at that time. He is therefore not only unable to warn the other animals of her presence but himself provides a sitting target:
> I must strike him in the daytime. The accursed one!
> I must root him out and exterminate him with my bite (p. 18).

Indeed, she subsequently finds the owl before dark, prepares to attack but at the last minute is diverted by the arrival of Philomel who now engages her full attention (p. 30).

Philomel, himself, can also be regarded as her helper: by singing to her, he enables her to be released from her curse.

The Opponent

Any actor, (including objects, abstract qualities or emotions) that hinders the subject in its quest is known as the opponent. Unlike the anti-subject (see pp. 49-50), the opponent does not have a quest of its own. In an athlete's attempt to acquire a gold medal at the Olympics, for example, physical fatigue and age may function as opponents.

In our story, night-time may be considered an opponent to the snake, Chea: Vigo is awake during these hours and therefore in a position to warn everyone of her presence.

If an opponent possesses a quest of its own, it becomes what is known as an anti-subject. Let us now discuss this term in greater detail.

The Anti-Subject

A story may contain two or more subjects whose quests are in opposition. An anti-subject is a subject, who, to achieve its goal, obstructs the quest of another subject. In the fight for a territory, for example, two opposing armies may each take up the positions of subject or of anti-subject, depending on the point of view from which the happenings are reported.

There are three principal types of situation in which an anti-subject might appear:

1. Two subjects, **SA** and **SB** are pursuing the same object or goal: **OA=OB**. If **SA** takes possession of the object or achieves its goal, it causes the quest of **SB** to fail and vice-versa. **SA** and **SB** are therefore anti-subjects. The two teams in a football match are in this relationship of anti-subject to each other as they are both in pursuit of the same object, namely, victory. Two countries at war are in a similar position.

The situation may be expressed in the following diagram:

The arrows on the clear lines convey the relationship subject-object. The dotted line conveys the relationship of anti-subject.

2. Two subjects, **SA** and **SB**, take each other as object. The prototype for this situation is a dual with pistols:

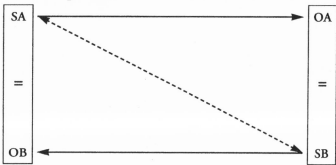

3. A subject, **SA**, takes another subject, **SB**, as object, **OA**. This second subject, **SB**, however, is pursuing its own object, **OB**, and refuses to be the object **OA** for **SA**. **SB**, therefore, opposes the quest of **SA**. When the quest of one of the subjects succeeds, the other fails:

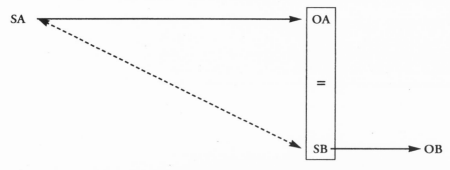

There are many examples of this third type of anti-subject in the story of Philomel. Chea's (**SA**) aim, for instance, is to destroy the life of Donna (**OA**) (pp. 17-18) whereas Donna's (**SB**) aim is to preserve it (**OB**). Similarly, Donna, **SA**, wants to protect the life of Philomel (**OA**) whereas Philomel (**SB**) wants to sacrifice it (**OB**). On page twenty-six, Lady Squirrel (**SA**) goes in pursuit of Philomel (**OA**) but the latter (**SB**) is only interested in his freedom (**OB**):

> And Lady Squirrel started to come down from the boughs to the trunk and from the trunk to reach the ground at such a speed that Philomel had scarcely time to fly onto a low branch and from there to another one higher until he arrived at his nest (p. 26).

In the discussion of narrative roles. I have so far focussed on the couples subject/object and helper/opponent (including the anti-subject). I shall now complete the actantial model with the introduction of two further roles, those of *sender* and *receiver*, situated on the axis of communication.

The Axis of Communication

The Sender

The sender represents the person or idea that motivates an action or causes something to happen. It not only institutes the values to be aimed for but also transmits the desire or obligation to a subject to pursue them. We call the desire or obligation to act the *modalities*. What is known as a *contract* is established between sender and receiver. The receiver, now in possession of one (or both) of these modalities is transformed into a subject ready to embark on a quest.

In their quest to defeat the Argentinians, the soldiers who took part in the Falklands war had two senders :

a) an external sender in the figures of Mrs Thatcher and of the British Government.

b) an internal sender in the belief in patriotism and in the traditional ideology of warfare.

In Philomel's first quest —the quest for knowledge— the sender can be described as curiosity and a sense of adventure. These emotions are implied in the opening conversation with Donna (p. 17), in the episode when he leaves the nest (p. 25) and later after he has learnt to fly (p. 28).

The actant Vigo could be said to hold the position of sender in Philomel's second and principal quest —to sing to Chea and to rid the world of evil. It is the information that Vigo gives to the nightingale about Chea (p. 28) that implants in him the desire to embark on this course of action. Philomel is also internally motivated by a moral concern for the welfare of others:

> Mother, if I meet Chea and sing to her, she might get rid of the poison in her mouth and become the King's daughter once again. And so the world below us will be freed from her evil.

His mother replies:

> Philomel! Get it out of your mind!
> What does the world below us matter to you? (p. 30).

Chea's impulses, on the other hand, are less altruistic. Her sender in her quest to be released from her curse and become the King's daughter once again is a sense of despair ('And Chea's days are filled with despair' p. 21), of personal loss associated with the memory of a former state.

The Receiver

The receiver represents the actant to whom a desire or obligation is given by a sender. This process or transaction must take place before the receiver can embark on a quest ie. before the receiver can assume the role of a subject. In the Falklands war, once the soldier/receiver decided to accept his mission or contract to go and fight, he became the subject of a quest (or global narrative programme).

Philomel is the receiver of the desire –transmitted by Vigo– to see Chea. He thus becomes the subject (virtual) of a narrative programme. Similarly, in the episode where Chea, the King's daughter, goes to the marshes (pp. 20-21) the desire and obligation to leave the Forest is transmitted by the Ogre –the sender– and she becomes the receiver. Having accepted the contract, that is, having decided to follow her desires or let herself be persuaded, she now assumes the role of subject of a quest.

After outlining in detail Greimas's actantial schema, I now propose to present a second narrative model, known as the *canonical narrative schema* or *the global narrative programme of the quest*. This schema conveys a series of logical phases through which all human action must pass.

The Canonical Narrative Schema
or
Global Narrative Programme of the Quest

It is clear that the distribution of actantial (narrative) roles in a story corresponds to the different stages of a global narrative programme. The sender and receiver, for example, play a key role in the initial stage of such a programme: this stage is known as the contract (or stage of manipulation). They also participate in the final stage, that is, at the stage of sanction or the *glorifying test*. The two intermediary stages relating directly to the action are termed the *stage of competence* or *the qualifying test* and the *stage of performance* or *the decisive test*.

These stages foreground the relationship **subject/object**.

All completed stories enact the above stages. This does not mean, however, that each stage is given equal weighting in a narrative: some are rendered explicit ie. manifested on the surface of the text whereas others are simply implied. In a conventional fairy tale, adventure story or thriller, for example, it is the stage of performance that is foregrounded whereas in many modern novels the focus is rather on the acquisition of competence (the qualifying test). Indeed, it will become evident that our chosen text, *Philomel*, also deviates in this respect from standard narrative patterns.

It must not be forgotten that many stories (global narrative programmes) remain incomplete: the hero/heroine may never progress to the decisive test, the quest may be terminated through a failure to acquire the necessary competence or through the arrival on the scene of a strong anti-subject. The logic, therefore, is one that operates in reverse ie, the completion of the performance or decisive test must necessarily imply the acquisition of competence which in turn implies the establishment of a contract (the stage of manipulation).

The Canonical Narrative Schema

contract	competence	performance	sanction
	qualifying test	*decisive test*	*glorifying test*
persuasive doing of sender			
acquisition of a wanting-to-do or a having-to-do	strengthening of desire	the primary event where object of value is at stake	subject is recognised
	acquisition of a being-able-to-do and/or of a knowing-how-to-do		success/failure praise/blame

Contract

This represents the initial stage of a global quest where the seeds of a future narrative programme are sown. Before embarking on a course of action, the subject must be persuaded to do so (something must cause it to act): it must either want to do something or feel obliged to do something. In semiotic terms, the subject must have acquired the modalities of virtuality, that is, a *wanting-to-do* or a *having-to-do*. If the goal of my quest is to successfully pass four 'A' levels, I could be motivated by a strong internal desire or ambition (a wanting-to-do) and also by an obligation transmitted by my parents (a having-to-do).

As we have seen, these modalities are communicated to the future subject by a sender and the relationship between the two is contractual. Two types of contract are possible:

I. *An Injunctive Contract*

Here the sender orders the future subject to do something. Many James Bond films open with such a contract: the hero is usually summoned and entrusted with a mission. In the episode where Chea is lured to the Marshes, the sentences 'I cannot, I cannot leave the Forest. I must never leave the Forest' (p. 20) imply that an injunctive contract has been established with her husband: she has been forbidden or ordered not to do something.

II. *A Permissive Contract*

Here the receiver or future subject asks permission to embark on a quest. Before visiting his friends in Newcastle, a boy may, for example, ask permission of his parents.

Once a contract has been established, the subject is ready to embark on a quest. In order to complete this quest, the subject must carry out three tests: *the qualifying test, the decisive test* and *the glorifying test.* These tests correspond to the stages of *competence*, of *performance* and of *sanction*.

Competence   or *the Qualifying Test*

This is the stage at which competence is acquired. By competence, we mean that the subject should be in possession of two attributes or qualifications. It must possess:

a) The desire or obligation to act (a wanting-to-do and/or a having-to-do).

These modalities have been transmitted by the sender but they can subsequently be strengthened or challenged in an episode or series of episodes. The subject could lose heart, for example, and give up the quest.

b) The ability to act (a being-able-to-do).

In order to be fully competent, the subject must also acquire the modality of *being-able-to-do*: it is not sufficient just to want to do something. This ability could be provided by a helper: if the aim of your quest is to obtain four Grade A's at 'A' Level, then the teachers will be your helpers, providing the necessary skills. The helper here could also be an object: money, for example, frequently provides the ability to act.

Sometimes this ability to act is closely linked with a knowledge of how to act, a *knowing-how-to-do*. In order to fly, a pilot not only needs an aeroplane but also a knowledge of how to operate the controls.

Performance   or *the Decisive Test*

The decisive test is the moment (episodes) in which the object of the quest is at stake, it is the principal event(s) towards which the story has been leading. In our example of the student seeking four grade A's, the decisive test (or performance) is the actual sitting of the examination.

In many stories, the decisive test takes the form of a confrontation with an anti-subject: if the goal is to acquire treasure, for example, the decisive test might be the killing of the dragon who guards the gold. In a competition such as an examination, the participants are in a necessary relationship of anti-subject to each other.

Sanction   or *the Glorifying Test*

The final phase of a global narrative programme is that of the sanction. Here the outcome of an event is being revealed, we learn whether the decisive test has succeeded or failed, the hero/heroine is acclaimed or punished, the action is deemed good or evil. In other words, it is the stage at which the performance is interpreted either by the narrator or an actor in the story. The person doing the interpreting is known as the sender-adjudicator: s/he judges whether the performance of the subject is in accordance with the original set of values established by the first sender (known also as the *mandating sender*) and whether the contract has been fulfilled or not. The role of sender –adjudicator can be held by two different actors or by the same person– you could, for instance, be judging your own actions.

In traditional fairytales the stage of sanction is frequently enacted in the figure of marriage: the father may reward the hero for his achievements (killing the dragon, for instance) by giving him his daughter's hand in marriage. In our example, the student who has sat the 'A' levels learns the results (sanction) and may also feel happy and be congratulated by others. Inversely, s/he may feel depressed and others might show their disappointment. Both the outcome and the reaction constitute the glorifying test.

The Global Narrative Programme of the Nightingale, Philomel

If we step back from the text and reconstruct a macronarrative or global story around the actor, Philomel, his principal quest becomes:

a) to see Chea (p. 28)
b) to sing to her and rid the world of evil (p. 30).

The following narrative schema emerges:

The Contract

a) The owl Vigo kindles Philomel's curiosity and imparts the desire to see the snake, Chea (pp. 27-28)
b) Vigo also imparts to Philomel the knowledge of how she can be released from her curse (p. 28).

The reader is left uncertain as to whether the decision to rid the world from evil was also made at this point: the desire is not verbally expressed until later when Philomel refuses to migrate with the birds (p. 30).

Competence   or *the Qualifying Test*

Competence is acquired and/or strengthened in the following episodes:
a) Philomel learns to fly (p. 25), and to sing (p. 28). He thus acquires the necessary being-able-to-do or knowing-how-to-do. His confidence increases ('the more he sang, the more confident he became and he started flying closer to the world below the trees').
b) Philomel acquires knowledge of the dangers of the world below and of how to survive in a hostile society. This knowledge is conveyed, for instance, in the encounter with Lady Squirrel (pp. 25-26) and with the Hare (p. 29). His desire to rid the world of conflict and evil is at the same time strengthened.

Performance   or *the Decisive Test*

The performance is enacted in the meeting with Chea (pp. 30-31). Philomel sings to Chea while taking flight. She pursues him and bites.

The Sanction   or *the Glorifying Test*

We learn that Philomel has been killed and that Chea has been released from her curse. His quest has thus been successful although it has cost him his life.

The Global Narrative Programme of the Snake Chea

The Stage of Contract

The memory of a former happier state together with the knowledge of how to regain this state (the Witch Faie tells her she must kill a bird while it is singing) kindle the desire to go on a quest.

Competence   or *the Qualifying Test*

a) She tries to kill Donna but fails.
b) She then attempts to kill Vigo who guards the Forest.
c) It is, however, Philomel himself who, in his desire to save Vigo, presents Chea with the favourable situation, that is, with the necessary being-able-to-do which she has lacked up to this point. It is he who helps her achieve her quest.

Performance   or *the Decisive Test*

The performance is enacted in the meeting with Philomel. He sings to her, she pursues and kills him.
It is to be noted that the actual death —and her ascent to the heavens— takes place offstage; the decisive test is not being foregrounded as would be the case in a more traditional fairy-tale.

The Sanction   or *the Glorifying Test*

We learn that Chea has shed her snakeskin and become a line of stars (p. 31). She too has been successful ln her quest.

This chapter has so far been concerned with the two fundamental narrative models, the actantial schema and the canonical narrative schema. These schemas give rise to a variety of complex patterns, a network of interacting narrative trajectories and transformations.

Indeed, according to C. Bremond[3], the story of any individual subject unfolds in a succession of phases of improvement and deterioration. A rich man may, for example, become poor (a process of deterioration or of becoming disjoined from an object of value) or a poor person rich (a process of improvement or of becoming conjoined with an object of value).

The choice of terms depends strictly on the point of view adopted by the narrator: what may be deterioration for one actor (character) —say **SA**— could be improvement for another — say **SB** :

Story	Perspective of SA	Perspective of SB
SA possesses **O**	+	−
SB seizes **O**	deterioration	improvement
SB possesses **O**	−	+

In the episode where Chea is lured to the marshes by the Ogre, what is a process of deterioration for her husband, the Son of Faie, is clearly one of improvement for the Ogre.

Story	Perspective of SA (husband)	Perspective of SB (Ogre)
SA ∩ **O** (Son of Faie married to Chea)	+	−
SB seizes **O** (Ogre lures Chea away)	deterioration	improvement
SB ∩ **O** (Ogre now possesses Chea)	−	+

The character favoured by the narrator is the Son of Faie: the text emphasises his loss rather than the Ogre's gain. It is this loss that triggers the next narrative programme, that is, the Witch Faie's curse on Chea.

This logic of narrative positions also means that at some point in a story two subjects must inevitably meet. This meeting will constitute a strategic point in the unfolding of the narrative. The arrival of the Son of Faie in the Marshes (followed by that of his helper, the Witch Faie) means that the object (Chea) is returned and that the narrative programmes of the Ogre and of Chea are abruptly brought to an end. This event triggers off a new story —Chea's life as a snake— and a new quest.

Transfer of the Object

The confrontation of subjects always results in the transfer of an object of value from one subject to another. This transfer could take three forms:

a) *transfer of the object by means of a test or conflict.*

The process here is one of appropriation and of deprivation. Before the meeting between the subjects **SA** may, for example, be conjoined with **O** :

$$\text{SA} \cap \text{O}$$

SB, then, would be *disjoined* from **O** :

$$\text{SB} \cup \text{O}$$

After meeting **SA**, is *disjoined* from **O** :

$$\text{SA} \cup \text{O}$$

SB is now *conjoined* from **O** :

$$\text{SB} \cap \text{O}$$

Before the Son of Faie (with his mother) arrives at the marshes, **SA** (the Ogre) is *conjoined* with the object (Chea) :

$$\text{SA} \cap \text{O}$$

SB (the Son of Faie) is *disjoined* from the object :

$$\text{SB} \cup \text{O}$$

After the meeting or confrontation, **SB** (the Son of Faie) is *conjoined* with the object (Chea) :

$$\text{SB} \cap \text{O}$$

SA (the Ogre) is *disjoined* from the object :

$$\text{SA} \cup \text{O}$$

It is **SB** (the Son of Faie) who seizes **O** (Chea) : the transfer of **O** is due to the initiative of **SB** who is a subject of doing :

$$\text{SB} \longrightarrow (\text{SA} \cup \text{O} \cap \text{SB})$$

This pattern of appropriation/deprivation need not always apply : objects can also be transferred by means of a gift.

b) *transfer of an object by means of a gift*

In some cases a subject (**SA**) may renounce an object and give it to someone else (**SB**):

$$SA \longrightarrow (SA \cup O \cap SB)$$

Greimas states:[4]

> If we give the name test to the transformation giving rise to an appropriation or to a deprivation, and the name gift to that which produces an attribution or a renunciation, we obtain the two principal figures by means of which the communication of values is manifested on the surface.

A simple diagram can illustrate these basic paradigmatic relations of the story:

	Acquisition	*Deprivation*
Test	Appropriation	Dispossession
Gift	Attribution	Renunciation

As we have seen, the meeting between the snake Chea and Philomel combines both elements : for Chea (**SA**) the relationship is oppositional, she takes Philomel's life (**O**) and he (**SB**) loses it.

$$SA \longrightarrow (SA \cap O \cup SB)$$

For Philomel (**SB**), however, there is no real struggle : he gives or surrenders his life to her (the notion of sacrifice) :

$$SB \longrightarrow (SB \cup O \cap SA)$$

Thirdly and lastly, objects can also be transferred by means of an exchange.

c) *transfer of two objects by means of an exchange*

Before the meeting of subjects, subject **SA** possesses the object, O^1, whereas **SB** possesses the object O^2:

$$O^1 \cap SA \cup O^2 \qquad and \qquad O^1 \cup SB \cap O^2$$

A butcher (**SA**) possesses a piece of meat (O_1) and the customer (**SB**) possesses the sum of money (O^2) necessary to exchange it for the meat. After the exchange we have the following situation :

$$O^1 \cup SA \cap O^2 \qquad and \qquad O^1 \cap SB \cup O^2$$

If a person performs a brilliant cello solo at a concert, s/he might receive resounding applause from the audience. Here the object, applause, is being exchanged for the feat of playing brilliantly.

Let us look at the episode where the Ogre promises Chea his treasure if she will go with him to the Marshes. The objects exchanged here can be considered Chea's own body (O^1) and the treasure (O^2).

Before meeting:

$$\mathbf{SA} \cap O^1 \qquad\qquad \mathbf{SB} \cap O^2$$

After meeting:

$$O^1 \cup \mathbf{SA} \cap O^2 \qquad O^1 \cap \mathbf{SB} \cup O^2$$

Interruption of the Narrative Programme of the Subjects

So far I have been examining the relationship that two subjects can have with an object: the meeting of subjects can lead to a transfer of objects by means of a test (struggle), a gift or an exchange. If, however, the object that is being sought by a subject, **SA**, is another subject, **SB**, then their meeting (presuming **SA** is successful) will result in the termination or interruption of the narrative programme of **SB**. **SB** will then adopt the role of object in the narrative programme of **SA**. The movement of **SB** from one narrative programme to another can be the result of an act of force or an act of persuasion on the part of **SA**. As we have seen, it is the physical intervention of the Son of Faie and his mother that puts an end to the narrative programmes of both Chea and the Ogre.

The principal aim of this chapter has been to present and illustrate the basic methodological tools enabling us to explore the narrative of a text. These tools are a fundamental requisite for those intending to undertake a semiotic analysis. I now propose to broaden my study to include two additional components, the figurative, and the thematic (or abstract). It is a fundamental postulate of semiotics that texts operate at more than one level[5]: as previously stated, the narrative level is situated mid-way between the figurative –the most concrete– and the deep level – the most abstract.

Notes to Chapter One

1. An analysis of extracts from this novel has been undertaken by J. Courtés, *Sémantique de l'énoncé: applications pratiques,* Paris, Hachette, 1989 and by N. Everaert-Desmedt, *Sémiotique du récit,* Bruxelles, De Boeck Université, 1989.

2. See A. J. Greimas, *Sémantique structurale,* Paris, Larousse, 1966, pp.172-221 for a discussion of the fundamental narrative schemas. An English translation is available (see bibliography).

3. See 'La logique des possibles narratifs' in *Communications*, nº 8, Le Seuil, 1966, Paris pp. 60-76.

4. *Languages,* nº 31, pp. 28-29.

5. Some semioticians operate with four levels – the fourth being known as the textual level. At this level we are concerned with questions of style: the use of metaphor, rhetorical devices etc.

Chapter Two

The Figurative Level

What is the figurative level?

The figurative level is the most concrete level of meaning: it relates to individual characters -known as actors- and to specific events unfolding in a given space and time. In other words, figurative elements are those elements in a text that correspond to the physical world and that can be apprehended by the *five senses*: vision, hearing, smell, taste and touch. It can be contrasted with the inner world of the conceptual or abstract, that is, with the third and deep level of meaning.

Figurativity clearly plays a key role in literature: it is at this level that the impression of the real world or referential illusion is constructed: the reader can never be in any doubt as to the authenticity of the fictive universe.

How do we analyse the figurative level?

Let us begin by looking closely at the surface of the text, that is, at the choice of vocabularly or lexical items. Can we group together those words that have a meaning in common or a common denominator?

These groupings are known as lexical fields or figurative isotopies. The words *house, shop, car* and *factory*, for instance, belong to the *isotopy of the city*. Similarly, *rain, wind* and *sun* belong to the *isotopy of the cosmic*.

When extracting the most important figurative isotopies from a literary text, it may be helpful to concentrate initially on notations relating to *space* (or *place*), to *time* and to the *characters*. Our attention will be drawn in particular to those items that repeat themselves.

Dominant figurative isotopies in the story of Philomel

Looking at the story as whole, the following groupings become apparent: the lists are by no means exhaustive and the reader may wish to add items and construct further isotopies.

Isotopy of the Forest

leaf(leaves) shrivelled leaf (p. 17), light– makes through the leaves (p. 25), tired of holding their leaves (p. 29)

grass crawl lazily in the grass (p. 23), low in the grass (p. 24)

bush (es) a bush became his hiding place (p. 19), from bush to bush (p. 23), and bushes (p. 28)

bough high up, on a bough (p. 25), from bough to bough (p. 26), from the boughs to the trunk (p. 26)

branch (es) onto a low branch (p. 26), on the branch of the linden tree (p. 28), low spreading branches (p. 28), landed on a branch (p. 29), sat on a branch (p. 30)

nest on the rim of the nest (p. 25), out of the nest (p. 25), he arrived at his nest (p. 26)

tree (s) on the trunk of the linden tree (p. 17), the world below the trees (p. 28), below the high trees (p. 29), when trees (p. 29), the canopy of the linden tree (p. 30), heading for your tree (p. 30), tree–abode (p. 31)

In addition to these notations, the word *Forest*, itself, appears on numerous occasions in the text (approximately twenty-one times!)

Isotopy of the Marshes

marshes down in the Marshes (p. 19), down in these Marshes (p. 20), into the Marshes (p. 20), in the Marshes (p. 20, twice), to the Marshes (p. 21, twice)

reeds amongst the reeds (p. 19), the reeds of the marshes (p. 20), reeds around her whispered (p. 20), in the depths, amongst the reeds (p. 21)

mire from the mire (p. 20), filthy from the mire (p. 21) filthy as when you emerged from the mire (p. 21)

muddy waters muddy waters and rotten leaves (p. 19), muddy waters (p. 21)

Isotopy of the Cosmic

Moon the Moon will rise (p. 17, twice), what is the Moon? (p. 17) you'll see the Moon tonight (p. 17), the Moon rises (pp. 17, 18), the

Moon is looking for me (p. 18), by the light of the Moon (pp. 18, 19), the Moon rises (p. 19), together with the Moon (p. 23) rose the Moon (p. 24), wandering like the Moon (p. 27)

Sky from the sky (p. 18), rises in the sky (p. 19), in accordance with the order of the sky (p. 23), high in the sky (p. 24), in the middle of the sky (p. 25), a honking noise from the sky (p. 30), in the azure of the sky (p. 30) rise into the sky (p. 31), his head to the sky (p. 31), high in the sky (p. 31)

Stars the stars had come out one by one (p. 23), they used to be stars once (p. 23), a line of shining stars (p. 31), amongst the other stars (p. 31)

Isotopy of Time

Day in the daytime (p. 19, twice), all day (pp. 20, 21, 28), one day (pp. 20, 25) that day (p. 20, twice), in those days (p. 18), since those far-off days (p. 21), and Chea's days (p. 21) movements of the Day (p. 23), the Days passed (p. 28), the Days were passing by (p. 29)

Twilight the twilight hour (p. 23) at this hour (p. 23), when the light of the day ends (p. 24), in the half light (p. 24) as the light dimmed (p. 31), but it is not yet dark (p. 30)

Night will father sing tonight? (p. 17), this evening when it is dark (p, 17), the night will come (p. 17), you'll see the Moon tonight (p. 17), all night long (p. 17), the Night's Sentinel (pp. 18, 19), night-time or not (p. 18), and one night, the kind of night (p. 19), on a night like this (p. 19) one night he leapt (p. 19), they croak all night (p. 19), mysteries of the Night begin (p. 23), to spend the night (p. 23), who sings all night (p. 23), into the darkness (p. 23), through the darkness (p. 23), one night without malice (p. 24), floated with the night (p. 24), and the Nights followed (p. 28), in the first shadows of the Night (p. 31).

Seasons either April/or May (p. 19), celebrated for a month (p. 19) for the whole month (p. 19), Autumn was approaching (p. 30)

In addition to place and time, there are two further dominant lexical fields. These can be termed the *isotopy of animals* and the *isotopy of fairy tale creatures*. For the sake of brevity, page references alone will be given.

Isotopy of Animals

birds: nightingales (pp. 17, 19, 23, 24, 25, 28, 30), birds of the Forest (pp. 18, 23), owl (pp. 18, 19, 23, 30, 31), hawk (p. 21), magpie (p. 20), geese (p. 30)

snake: snake (pp. 17, 18, 21, 23, 27), tree-snakes (p. 18), water-snakes (p. 18), serpent (p. 31)

insects: butterflies (p. 19), bees (p. 20), fireflies (pp. 23, 31), may-beetle (p. 24), grasshoppers (p. 29), spiders (p. 27), insects (p. 27), worms (p. 27), ants (p. 31)

other animals: squirrel (pp. 25, 26), hare (pp. 27, 29), weasels (pp. 18, 27), martens (p. 27), foxes (pp. 27, 29), ferrets (pp. 27, 29), wolf (p. 29), frogs (pp. 19, 20).

Isotopy of Fairy Tale Creatures

fairies and goblins (pp. 18, 19), daughter of a King (King's daughter) (pp. 18, 21, 28, 30), maidens (pp. 18, 19), Son of Faie (pp. 19, 20, 21), Witch Faie (pp. 20, 21), Ogre (pp. 20, 21).

The above list of items is by no means exhaustive. The reader, for example, may also choose to examine the *isotopy of movement* (in particular notations relating to upward and downward movement) and the *isotopy of sound* (including references to singing and to speech). The selection of isotopies (and they cannot all be listed) will inevitably be determined by the overall focus or aim of the semiotic analysis. If our goal for example, is to examine mythical elements in the story, then we shall concentrate only on those items that are pertinent to our argument.

The Figurative Level and Oppositions

Meaning is not simply the product of repetition. As Saussure has said 'there is no meaning without difference'.[1]

Having extracted the most important isotopies, we must now ask ourselves: what are the key oppositions that emerge at this level? Which oppositions dominate?

Looking carefully at our lists, we are struck by the recurrence of terms relating to height and depth. The following inventory could be drawn up:

high	low
the Moon will rise (p. 17, twice)	down below, in the Forest (p. 23)
and rise high into the sky to seek her husband (p. 21)	
they (the Fireflies) used to be stars once (p. 23)	that fell to earth (p. 23)
the time will come for them to ascend . . . high in the sky (pp. 23-24)	
they would rise high (p. 24)	creatures . . . jump in the world below (p. 27)
and higher than the trees escalated the voice . . . it was raised to be heard in the heavens (p. 24)	
in the Forest exist two worlds: . . . the one above (p. 27)	in the Forest exist two worlds: the one below (p. 27)
Vigo flew . . . to his lofty abode (p. 28)	searched for Chea over the floor of the world below (p. 28)
	started flying closer to the world below the trees (p. 28)
	in the world below the high trees, over the floor of the Forest (p. 29)
	he looked down to ground: Philomel lay lifeless (p. 31)
serenity reigned high in the trees and higher in the sky (p. 31)	peace had nestled in the world below (p. 31)

The spatial setting of the story of *Philomel* is characterised, therefore, by the fundamental opposition high **vs** low, the world above the trees being compared, for instance, to the world below the trees. There are, however, further spatial divisions within the text whose significance cannot be ignored. The world above the trees, for example, –associated with the birds– is contrasted with the world of the sky (higher in the sky)– associated with the stars and the timeless. Similarly, the world below the trees includes (and at one point contrasts with) the lower world of the Marshes.

These spatial oppositions do not signify in themselves; they only acquire meaning when read in conjunction with the narrative and deep(thematic) levels. A process of correlation, therefore, takes place. I shall begin by looking at the quests.

The Quest of Chea

a) the figurative level and the narrative

If we look at the global narrative programme or quest of Chea, the space of the 'world below' (and of the Marshes) can be correlated with a state of disjunction. The curse of Witch Faie (p. 21) produces a lack or awareness of a missing state together with the desire to regain a lost object. This object of desire or goal of the quest is associated with the 'world above' (the seme of high) and with the figure of the sky: Chea's aim is to kill a bird while it is singing and thereby to 'become the King's daughter once again, and rise high into the sky to seek her husband' (p. 21). Spatial divisions are thus being invested with values, the 'high' being correlated with the *pleasant* or *euphoric* and the 'low' being correlated with the *unpleasant* or *dysphoric*:

$$\begin{array}{ccc} \text{high} & & \text{euphoric} \\ & = & \\ \text{low} & & \text{dysphoric} \end{array}$$

Indeed, contrary to the traditional notion of the 'real', the construction of a fictive universe or of the referential illusion can never take place independent of a subjective process of evaluation. What is known as the *thymic category* –the category relating to feelings and moods (euphoric **vs** dysphoric)– must always come into play occupying a central role in the production of meaning.

b) the figurative level and the thematic

The 'world below' and 'down below' is clearly linked thematically with the concept of evil. The episode where Chea is tempted down to the Marshes, for instance, recalls the myth of the Fall and the Biblical curse: Chea is condemned to crawl on her belly and to spread poison:

> you will crawl on your belly and whatever you eat
> from your mouth will be poisoned (p. 21)

She is a key factor in the conflict in the Forest and a never-ending source of fear:

> Everyone is trained by fear down here and everybody dreads Chea (p. 29)

The success of her quest, her rising to the sky, means that she has achieved a personal redemption or salvation. It has also brought peace on earth. The following correlations can, therefore, be made:

$$high = salvation = peace$$

$$low = damnation = conflict$$

The association of the high with the positive and spiritual (notions of Heaven and of Paradise) and the low with the negative and evil (concept of Hell) is, of course, archetypal. The reader may be reminded here of the works of the French philosopher, Gaston Bachelard.[2]

The Quest of the Fireflies

A similar spatial programming characterises the quest of the fireflies. They, too, have experienced a lack, a disjunction from a former state (that of being stars) and it is this memory of Eden that triggers the quest:

> They used to be stars once, the Fireflies say, that fell to earth...
> They assume the time will come for them to ascend once again,
> to where they belong, high in the sky.

Thematically, this ascent is linked with the passage from *evil* to *good*. The text continues:

> They say one night without malice in the Forest would suffice,
> then they would rise high... (pp. 23-24)

Chea's rising into the sky and transformation into a 'line of shining stars' (p. 14) means that they too will be saved:

At last we will rise into the sky! High up above where Chea has gone (p. 31)

The Quest of Philomel

As a young bird Philomel is associated with the figure of the nest and with the world above the trees – a positive and euphoric space. As he grows, however, his quest for knowledge takes him closer to the world below the trees (p. 28). This world below is essentially dysphoric and linked with the themes of danger (the episode with Lady Squirrel (pp. 25, 26), conflict and strife:

So they (the ants) advised him to be vigilant because,
in the world below the high trees, over the floor of the Forest,
there are many vicious enemies (p. 29)

Indeed, the world below is evoked as being in constant conflict with the world above to which it seeks to do the utmost harm (p. 27). The awareness of this state of affairs awakens in Philomel a profound dissatisfaction and triggers what will become his principal quest: to rid the world of evil and conflict by singing to Chea (p. 30). This quest must necessarily be enacted in the world below. As we have seen, Philomel achieves his goal although at the cost of his own life ('on the ground with wings outstretched, Philomel lay lifeless'): the conflict is brought to an end and peace is restored to the Forest.

This theme of harmony is reinforced in the text in the figure of the nightingale's song which transcends all spatial boundaries to rise up into the cosmic, timeless space of the heavens (p. 24).

In this chapter I have outlined a number of key features of the figurative level and attempted to examine their role in the production of meaning. The analysis of the text is by no means comprehensive, my primary purpose being to present a methodology or analytical approach that can be applied to all texts.

Notes to Chapter Two

1. *Cours de Linguistique Générale,* Geneva, 1915, ed. Charles Bally, Albert Sechehaye and Albert Riedlinger. Translated by Wade Baskin: *Course in General Linguistics,* New York, 1959.

2. See in particular: *Poétique de l'espace,* P.U.F., Paris, 1957. An English translation exists, *The Poetics of Space,* Beacon Press.

Chapter Three

The Deep Level

After analysing the narrative and figurative levels of meaning, we go on to examine the deep level, known also as the thematic level. This is the level of the abstract or conceptual: it relates to the inner mental world as opposed to the outer physical world of the figurative level. It is the level at which are articulated the fundamental values of the text.

But how do we arrive at these values?

We begin by looking for the fundamental opposition(s) or transformation(s) underlying the text. To help us in this task, it may be helpful to ask the following questions:

a) Can we reduce all the oppositions we have found on the figurative and narrative level to one or two basic umbrella oppositions that can function as a common denominator for the rest?

b) What are the two most abstract poles of meaning between which the text moves?

c) What fundamental transformation(s) of values is at stake?

Looking back at the analysis of the story of *Philomel* in Chapters *One* and *Two*, two underlying thematic oppositions clearly emerge. These are:

conflict **vs** harmony

damnation **vs** salvation

These oppositions can now be presented in the form of a semiotic square. But what exactly is a semiotic square?

The Semiotic Square

The semiotic square is the visual presentation of this fundamental opposition(s) and of the transformation from one pole to its opposite. It was originally devised by A. J. Greimas. In the interests of practibility, I shall only be presenting the bare outlines of this square. I shall begin with the two opposite terms, (**s¹** and **s²**).

Let us take the example: **s¹**   **s²**
                                   life   death

s¹ and **s²** are in opposition or in a relationship of contrariety. In order to be in a relationship of contrariety, the two terms must have one feature in common (or a common denominator). For instance, 'life' and 'death' have 'state of being' in common. According to Greimas, two terms can be considered contraries if the one presupposes the other.

But, logically, you cannot move directly from **s¹** to **s²**. In order to move from **s¹** to **s²** you must first of all negate **s¹**, that is, you must move to non **s¹** (**-s¹**), the contradictory term. In our case, we move from 'life' to 'non-life':

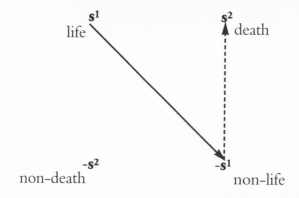

Similarly, if you are at **s²** you must move to **s¹** via non **s²** (**-s²**). In our case, we move from 'death' to 'non-death' (e.g. the story of Christ's resurrection). And non **s²** ('non-death') usually implies **s¹** ('life'). From negation, therefore, you move to assertion and a complete square emerges:

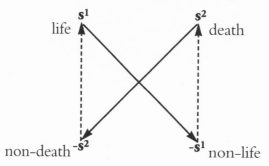

If we look at the story of *Philomel*, the following semiotic square can be constructed:

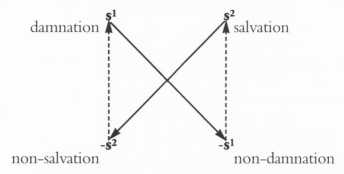

Adopting the perspective of Chea, her main quest begins after the curse and her transformation into a snake. Her trajectory, then, commences at s^1, presented as a state of damnation. She desires to move away from this original state by biting a bird whilst it is singing. Her meeting with Philomel (pp. 30-31) provides her with the opportunity; the episode marks, therefore, the negation of her original position and she now moves to $-s^1$ (non-damnation). At this point she also rises into the sky to become a star: $-s^1$ implies, then, s^2 ie, her salvation:

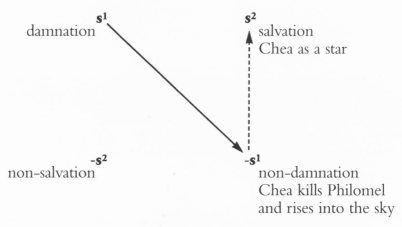

To summarise, we could say that, expressed in its most abstract form, Chea's initial state is one of damnation (s^1) and that her final state is one of salvation (s^2). The transformations in her story are enacted at $-s^1$, the point where her original position is being negated. If, of course, we were to include her pre-history and begin at **s²** when she was a King's daughter, then her narrative trajectory would go full circle, occupying all four points of the semiotic square:

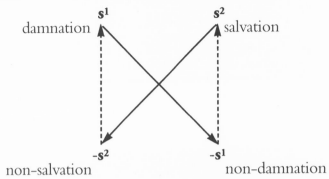

This fundamental movement from damnation to salvation is paralleled by a second opposition of equal importance, that is, the transformation from a state of conflict to a state of harmony. This change of state characterises the whole Forest and is experienced by all the actors in the story:

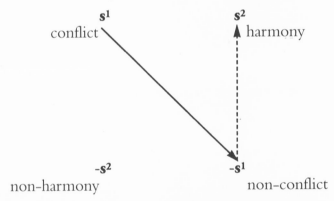

In the chapter on figurativity I showed how the values of damnation and of conflict were linked with the world below and those of salvation and of harmony with the world above and the sky. The story ends, therefore, with the victory of the world above and the assertion of positive values.

Text and Context

Having ascertained the fundamental abstract values underlying the text, we must now open our analysis to include broader considerations of cultural influence (including intertextuality) and of socio-political context and function. It would be helpful, therefore, to ask ourselves the following questions:

a) Where do the values in the text come from? With what tradition (or intellectual movement) can they be linked?

b) What is the relationship of the text to dominant ideologies or value-systems (past and present)?
Does it challenge or strengthen the status quo?

c) What type of reader is implied (or constructed) by the text?

To help us answer some of these questions, I propose to outline a number of possible readings of the text. My aim is not to cover every aspect of the *Philomel* story (if that were possible!) but simply to suggest avenues for further study or research.

Philomel and the Mythic Tradition

a) *The Christian Story*

The enactment of the fundamental oppositions damnation **vs** salvation, conflict **vs** harmony, echoes the Christian story. The narrative trajectory of the two principal actors, Chea and Philomel, acquires additional significance when read in this light.

Chea

Chea was originally the daughter of a King who 'used to go dancing with the other maidens, by the light of the Moon' (p. 19) and who 'revelled in her dance' (p. 19). She can be likened here to Eve in the Garden of Eden who is described as sharing similar experiences of joy and of oneness with the environment. The expression 'daughter of a King' may also suggest her divine origins (King = God). This paradisaical state is not, however, permanent.

Her seduction by the Ogre (pp. 20-21) down to the Marshes and her transformation into a snake mirrors the story of the Fall and of God's curse on humankind. The text runs 'From now on... you will crawl on your belly (p. 21) and the Bible 'On your belly you will crawl' (Genesis 3). Beauty and light fade ('they (Chea's eyes) are dull and evil' (p. 27) and she is condemned to a life of despair ('And Chea's days are filled with despair' p. 21). The snake itself is a conventional symbol of evil in Christian mythology; Chea's own desire to regain a lost Paradise of beauty and joy (to become the King's daughter once again) can, therefore, be said to mirror humankind's own quest for an individual, personal salvation. This quest is also echoed in the story of the Fireflies who 'used to be stars once... that fell to earth' (p. 23).

Philomel

Philomel's own narrative trajectory can be likened to that of Christ who also gave his life to save humankind and to bring peace on earth. This notion of the sacrificial victim is of course common to several myths or cultures and pre-dates Christianity.

Philomel's desire to visit 'the world below the trees' and to acquire knowledge of evil can likewise be compared to Christ's mingling with ordinary people and with sinners. Through the power of song Philomel is also able to perform miracles, to transform evil into good.

b) *Non-Christian Myths*

The story of *Philomel* is clearly steeped in a wealth of myths drawn from a wide variety of different cultures. The image of the star, for example, would recall both Greek and Mayan myths (the stars are human souls) as does that of the serpent. The notion of transformation or metamorphosis is, of course, an ancient one. The nightingale is itself an archetypal symbol of beauty and perfection and gives rise to a variety of different stories in different cultures. As in Shakespeare's 'Romeo and Juliet', it is frequently associated with the themes of love and death.

At the same time, we are struck by the importance attached in the story of *Philomel* to the cosmic: events are situated in relationship to a circular cosmic time —to night and day, to light and darkness— rather than to linear historical time. The moon and stars also play a key role in the narrative. Indeed, the foregrounding of the cosmic at the end —in the figure of the star– can be seen as mirrowing a return to an original unity or oneness with creation. The text can thus be seen to embody traditional notions of the sacred.

Philomel and the Poetic Tradition (Orpheus).

In the story of *Philomel* our attention is frequently drawn to the image of the nightingale's song:

> Suddenly, in the profound silence of the Forest, the song of the Nightingale was heard. The wild violets who whisper when the light of the day ends and every fragrant whisper from them perfumes the air, yearned for the song in the half light; the little owl who every now and then stops his solitary chatter and pricks up an ear, longed to hear it; even the silent stream which flows so calmly as if it had stopped, craved for the song to begin.
> And higher than the trees escalated the voice of the Nightingale, scale by scale, it was raised to be heard in the heavens. And as the entire Forest listened to the song which floated with the Night, little by little, beyond the distant hills, rose the Moon. (p. 24)

Song is being associated here with beauty and with a yearning for perfection and for the sacred. Its effect, like that of Orpheus's lute, is to bring peace and harmony to the Forest; it is, of course, Philomel's singing to Chea that eventually frees the world below from evil. The nightingale's song can therefore be seen as a symbol of the redeeming power of art (and of beauty).

Philomel and the Children's Story

References to the King's daughter, the Witch Faie, the Ogre, and to maidens, fairies and goblins as well as to the motif of the curse suggest the influence of the traditional fairytale. Similarly, the allegorical use of animals recalls the tradition of the fable and we are reminded of texts such as Aesop's fables and R. Kipling's *Just So Stories*. This type of literature was written for children and adults alike.

A Socio-Political Reading of *Philomel*

a) *Gender*

If we look at the distribution of gender roles in the story, we are struck by the element of ambiguity. On the one hand, the text privileges the female in the figure of Chea. It is she (rather than Adam) who reenacts the myth of the Fall; and it is the female that subsequently becomes the symbol of humankind's suffering and quest to return to a paradisaical state. On the other hand we also note the following points:

1. Chea is tempted not to eat of the Tree of Knowledge but to acquire material wealth (the Ogre's treasures).

2. Chea is punished by her husband because she disobeyed him and left the Forest without his permission. Contemporary readers (including many children) consider this punishment either to be excessive or unjustified. The word treasure is, of course, ambiguous: on a deeper level it can be said that Chea is being punished by a patriarchal society for her affirmation of sexual freedom.

3. The text implicitly associates the female with evil (Chea) and the male with good (Philomel). The symbol of wisdom and knowledge —Vigo— is also male.

If we look at the text as a whole, we are indeed struck by the complexity of the characterisation. Unlike the traditional story, the villain or symbol of evil (Chea) is presented in a sympathetic light and the reader is led to identify with her. At the same time, the motivations of the hero Philomel are left ambiguous: did he really intend to sacrifice his life or did he hope to sing to Chea and escape unscathed? The gaps or ambiguities of the text allow readers space to interpret and to construct meanings that may reflect their own cultural heritage and assumptions.

b) *Socio-Political Activity*

The image of society presented in the text is one of conflict: the groups of animals seek to harm each other. Central importance is attached to the notion of fear which is presented as the single unifying or cohesive force:

> the circle of fear that binds all creatures to the same fate (p. 29).

The Hare comments:

> We live with fear in our hearts and we lose heart from fear
>
> and
>
> Everyone is trained by fear down here and everybody dreads Chea (p. 29)

Chea is described as the principal source of the social evil and it is only her metamorphosis that will bring this evil to an end. She can be likened symbolically to those forces (groups) within society who, in order to achieve their goal, must eradicate or eliminate others; in historical terms Chea could represent movements of totalitarianism. Indeed, the author, Ange S. Vlachos, may well have been thinking of the German occupation of Greece when he wrote the story in 1943.

In contrast, then, the figure of the nightingale Philomel can be said to mirror the following political attitudes:

1. a refusal to accept the status quo and to succumb to a universal fear.

2. a desire to make human society a better place.

3. a belief that the action of an individual can make a difference and that social conflict can be reduced through acts of selflessness.

4. a conviction that different peoples or groups can live together in harmony and peace.

> This chapter has brought to the fore the fundamental values underlying the text of *Philomel*. Whilst remaining firmly embedded within a structural framework that is universal, these values at the same time acquire a semantic specificity within their cultural and socio-political context. The semiotic approach has indeed made it possible for us to uncover a wealth of meanings hidden beneath the surface of a deceptively simple fairy tale.

Conclusion

The aim of this study has been to present readers with an example of the practical application of semiotic theory. I hope thereby to have provided a methodology that can be applied to all literary texts as well as to media items such as news stories and political speeches. This methodology has inevitably been simplified and I do not claim to have covered all aspects of semiotic theory. The question of enunciation, for example, has been omitted and will form part of a future publication. As well as providing a working model for textual analysis, therefore, I also hope that this book has sufficiently stimulated the reader to pursue further this most exciting area of human inquiry. At the same time, of course, the book serves as an introduction to the work of Ange S. Vlachos.

As we have already seen, semiotics is essentially the study of how meaning is produced. From this point of view it can be regarded as a new form of humanism and a challenge to many postmodernist assumptions.

In the opening page of *Structural Semantics* (see bibliography), A. J. Greimas states:

> It seems to me that the human world can be defined essentially
> as the world of meaning. The world can only be described
> as 'human' insofar as it means something.

Semiotics is concerned above all then with coherence, coherence being, as Greimas[1] says, one of those very few criteria for measuring truth that human kind has been able to devise.

---

1. *Du sens,* Paris, Seuil, 1970, p. 9

Semiotics: **Selected Bibliography**

Works in English:

Eco, U., *The Role of the Reader,* Bloomington, Indiana University Press, 1984

Martin, B., *The Search for Gold: Space and Meaning in J.M.G. Le Clézio,* Dublin, Philomel Productions Ltd., 1995

Greimas, A.J., *Structural Semantics,* Lincoln and London, Nebraska University Press, 1983

Greimas, A.J., *Maupassant. The Semiotics of Text,* translated by P. Perron, Amsterdam-Philadelphia, John Benjamins, 1988

Greimas, A.J., & Courtés, J., *Semiotics and Language,* An Analytical Dictionary, Bloomington, Indiana University Press, 1982

Hawkes T., *Structuralism and Semiotics,* London, Methuen, 1977

Perron, P. & Collins, F. (editors), *Paris School of Semiotics*: Volumes I & II Amsterdam-Philadelphia, John Benjamins, 1989

Works in French:

Arrivé, M. & Coquet, J.C., *Sémiotique en jeu. A partir et autour de l'œuvre d'A.J. Greimas,* Paris-Amsterdam, Hadès-Benjamins, 1987

Bertrand, D. *L'Espace et le sens. Germinal d'Emile Zola,* Paris-Amsterdam, Hadès-Benjamins, 1985

Coquet, J.C. (edited) *Sémiotique – Ecole de Paris,* Paris, Hachette, 1982

Courtés, J., *Introduction à la sémiotique narrative et discursive,* Paris, Hachette, 1976.

Courtés, J., *Analyse sémiotique du discours,* Paris, Hachette, 1991

Courtés, J., *Sémantique de l'énoncé: applications pratiques,* Paris, Hachette, 1989

Everaert-Desmedt, N., *Sémiotique du récit,* Bruxelles, De Boeck-Wesmael, 1989

Floch, J.M., *Petites mythologies de l'œil et de l'esprit. Pour une sémiotique plastique,* Paris-Amsterdam, Hadès-Benjamins, 1985

Floch, J.M., *Identités visuelles,* Paris, P.U.F., 1995

Floch, J.M., *Sémiotique, marketing et communication.* Paris, P.U.F., 1990

Fontanille, J., *Le savoir partagé. Sémiotique et théorie de la connaissance chez Marcel Proust*, Paris–Amsterdam, Hadès–Benjamins, 1987

Fontanille, J., *Les espaces subjectifs*, Paris, Hachette, 1989

Greimas, A.J., *Sémiotique structurale*, Paris, Larousse, 1966

Greimas, A.J., *Du sens*, Paris, Seuil, 1970

Greimas, A.J., *Du sens*, Volume II, Paris, Seuil, 1982

Greimas, A.J., *Maupassant, la sémiotique du texte, exercices pratiques*, Paris, Seuil, 1976

Greimas, A.J., *Sémiotique et sciences sociales*, Paris, Seuil, 1976

Greimas, A.J., *De l'imperfection*, Périgueux, Fanlac, 1987

Greimas, A.J., & Courtés, J., *Sémiotique. Dictionaire raisonné de la théorie du langage,* Paris, Hachette, 1979

Dáithí Ó hÓgáin

Dáithí Ó hÓgáin was born in Bruff, Co Limerick, Ireland, in 1949, and now resides in Bray, near Dublin, with his wife and five children. He studied at University College Dublin, where he was awarded a BA Degree in modern languages and an MA Degree in literature. In 1977 a Doctorate was conferred on him from the National University of Ireland. He has worked as an editor, journalist, and broadcaster, and has for many years been employed as a Senior Lecturer in Irish Folklore at University College Dublin. He served as Rapporteur-General at the conference in Paris in 1987 at which the Unesco policy on the safeguarding of folklore was drafted, and was co-chairman of the inaugural session of the European Center for Traditional Culture in Budapest in 1995. He is a well-known poet and writer of short stories in the Irish language, six volumes of his creative work having been published. In this context, he has lectured and given readings of his work in several countries, and has also edited five volumes of traditional poetry and song. He is the author of many analytical works on literature and folklore, most notably *An File* (1982 – a study of the traditional images of poets); *The Hero in Irish Folk History* (1985 – a study of the connections between history and myth); *Fionn Mac Cumhaill* (1988 – a study of Irish epic); and *Myth, Legend and Romance* (1990 – an encyclopaedia of traditional narrative in Ireland). Dr Ó hÓgáin is currently working on a study of prehistoric religion and on a new collection of his own poetry.

Bronwen Martin

Dr Bronwen Martin was born in Bermuda in 1946. She attended The Girls' Grammar School, Stevenage, from 1958-1964. She was awarded a B.A. Hons. in Modern Languages (French and German) at Manchester University in 1970. In 1980 she was awarded a M.A. in French and in 1990 a PhD (French) by London University. She taught modern languages in secondary schools from 1971-1985.

Dr Bronwen Martin lives in Bromley, Kent with her husband and two small children. At present she teaches European literature and Semiotics at Birkbeck College, London University. She also teaches discourse analysis at Middlesex University. Her most recent research includes the application of semiotics to media studies and to the analysis of medical and academic discourse. She is currently working on the completion of a semiotics dictionary and on a textbook for advanced learners of French. *Books*: co-author, *Living English: Thinking, Speaking, Writing*, ELM Publications, 1993. Sole author, *The Search for Gold: Space and Meaning in J.M.G. Le Clézio*, Philomel Productions Ltd, 1995 – *Articles: Space and Meaning: An Analysis of a Passage from J.M.G. Le Clézio's <<La Guerre>>*, La Chouette, Birkbeck College, 1986, *An Introduction to Semiotic Analysis*, La Chouette, Birkbeck College, 1995

Ange S. Vlachos

• Born in 1915 in Egypt • Graduated in Law, University of Athens, 1937 • Joined the Greek Diplomatic Corps in 1939 • *He was appointed to the following posts:* Vice-Consul to Constantinople • First Secretary to the Embassy in Rome • Consul General to Jerusalem and Cyprus • Permanent Delegate to the U.N.O., Geneva • Director of Cultural Affairs to the Foreign Ministry • Ambassador to Moscow • Secretary General to the Ministry of Foreign Affairs • Minister to the Prime Minister in the Karamanlis Government, 1974 • Director General of Radio-Television, Greece, 1975-76 • Member of the Academy of Athens, 1985

Books

1. *The Witch's Grave* (Albanian Campaign), 1945
2. *My Master Alcibiades* (historical novel), 1953, Ouranis Prize
3. *Hours of Life*, Prize of the Ministry of Education, 1958
   (fiction: a prisoner's life in the German camps during the Occupation)
4. *Their Most Serene Majesties* (historical novel), 1963
5. *Lucky Daimas* (short stories), Prize of the Ministry of Education, 1968
6. *Partialités chez Thucydide* (essay), 1970, in French
7. *Herodotus the Wronged* (essay), 1970
8. *A Philhellene in 1821* (the Greek War of Independence, historical novel)
   Prize of the Academy of Athens, 1972
9. *The 14th of Nizan*, 1972
10. *Pilgrims to Susa* (essay), 1973
11. *Green Moscow*, 1976
12. *Xerxes: Private Papers*
    (fictional portrait), 1978
13. *Ten years of Cyprus* (history), 1980
14. *The Ravings of Pythia*, 1983
15. *Once Upon a Time a Diplomat* (memoirs)
    6 Volumes   I   1985   III   1986   V   1987
             II   1985   IV   1986   VI   1988
16. *In Inverted Order,* (Prothysteron), 1983
17. *The King's Shadow*, 1991
18. *Tsoufis, a mythologema*, 1993
19. *Ecclesiastes*, 1994
20. *Commentaries on Thucydides*, 1994
21. *Lyrical Short Stories*, 1995
22. *The Intermittant Life of Dimitri Speris*, 1996

Translations

1. Thucydides, *The Peloponnesian War*, 1965, Book I-VIII
2. Herodotus, *The Histories*, 1972, Book I-IX
3. Aeschylus, *Prometheus Bound*, 1973
4. *The Gospels: Matthew, Mark, Luke, John*, 1977
5. A. Camus, *Calligula*, 1978
6. Aristoteles, *The Constitution of Athens*, 1980
7. G.M. Woodhouse, *The Greek War of Independence*, 1980
8. *Cavafy's: Poems*, 1981 (French), Silver Medal of the Académie Française
9. *The Acts of the Apostles*, 1985
10. Cavafy, *Inedited Poems* (Greek/French), 1995

Theatre

1. *The Belfry* (inspired by the life of the Russian architect Kovnir, XVIIth century)
2. *The Failure of a Resurrection* (the clandestine life of a communist during the Franco regime in Spain)
3. *The Sheep Merchant* (the second marriage of Aspasia)

Translated works of the author

1. *The Witch's Grave* (partly in French)
2. *Their most Serene Majesties* in English, published by Bodley Head, London 1963, the Vanguard Press, New York
3. *My Master Alcibiades,* in Romanian, published by Editura Univers, Bucharest, 1970
4. *Hours of Life* (translated into English by Peter Bien), published by "The Charioteer", New York, 1972
5. *Pilgrims to Sousa,* in Romanian, published by Editura Univers, Bucharest, 1976
6. *Ecclesiastes* in Catalan, English, French, Irish, Italian, Scottish-Gaelic, Spanish and Welsh, published by Philomel Productions Ltd in 1995
7. *Philomel, a modern Greek fable* (original title <<Tsoufis: a mythologema>>) published –in Irish and English– by Philomel Pros Ltd in 1993.

Paul S. Vlachos

painter

Paul S. Vlachos was born in Mansura, Egypt in 1921. He attended the School of Arts in Athens in 1943 and from 1947-50 he studied stage design at the 'Old Vic Theatre School' in London, U.K. Works of Paul S. Vlachos have been bought by the National Gallery, Athens, Greece and works of his can be found in private collections in Greece. He has designed the covers for the books of his brother, Ange S. Vlachos, *Lucky Daimas, The 14th of Nizan, Pilgrims to Susa, The Gospels: Matthew, Mark, Luke, John, Philomel, Ecclesiastles*

- *Philomel, a modern Greek fable* (original title <<*Tsoufis, a mythologema*>>, written in 1943). Published by Philomel Pros Ltd –in Irish, English and Greek– in 1993.

All 3 hardback editions were illustrated with 130 (four-coloured) drawings by the Greek painter and sculptor, Christos Georgiou. Paul S. Vlachos (at the age of 26) was the first artist whose illustrations fully interpreted the story of *Philomel*. Drawings and pictures were sold –through the years– at various exhibitions. Except for the designs of the bookcover, only two illustrations remain in his possession, one print of which has been included in all 3 hardback versions published in 1993. The book, *Semiotics and Storytelling,* by Bronwen Martin, with a foreword by Dáithí Ó hÓgáin, published in 1997, is illustrated with the original designs by Paul S. Vlachos made in 1947 for the story of *Philomel,* written by his brother in 1943

- *Ecclesiastes (*a personal rendering of the original Greek text of *Ecclesiastes* –Chapter III– by Ange S. Vlachos). The Greek version was published by Philomel Pros Ltd in 1994 .

In 1993, Paul S. Vlachos designed the Greek bookcover and text of *Ecclesiastes*. In 1994 he designed the bookcovers for *Ecclesiastes* in Catalan, English, French, Irish, Italian, Scottish-Gaelic, Spanish and Welsh. His illustrations of the Greek edition were used in all 8 versions. They were published by Philomel Pros Ltd in 1995

- *The Search for Gold: Space and Meaning in J. M. G. Le Clézio,* a critical study of four of Le Clézio's works, by Bronwen Martin. Published by Philomel Pros Ltd in 1995

In this book Dr Martin presents her analysis of the four works of J. M. G. Le Clézio in four consecutive chapters. Paul S. Vlachos's visual interpretations accompany each chapter and make this academic book a real pleasure to possess and to read

Typesetting by
The Meeting House
1 North Farm Road, Tunbridge Wells
Kent TN2 3DH
Tel: ++44 (0)1892 54 40 88
Fax: ++(0)1892 54 69 21

Printed and bound in Greece by
EUROPRINT
Ath. E. Petroulakis S.A.
3km Koropi – Vari Av.
19400, Athens, Greece
Tel: ++ 30 1 602 22 42-5/602 00 11
Fax: ++ 30 1 662 39 57

Designed by **Sophia Kakkavas**

1997